Men
at Work

Life beyond the Office

James E. Dittes

Westminster John Knox Press
Louisville, Kentucky

Scripture quotations are from *Good News Bible: The Bible in Today's English Version.* Old Testament: © American Bible Society, 1976; New Testament: © American Bible Society, 1966, 1971, 1976.

Book design by Gene Harris
Cover design by Vickie Arrowood

Second edition
This book was originally published as *When Work Goes Sour: A Male Perspective*

Published by Westminster John Knox Press
Louisville, Kentucky

This book is printed on acid-free paper that meets the American National Standards Institute Z39.48 standard. ∞

PRINTED IN THE UNITED STATES OF AMERICA

95 96 97 98 99 00 01 02 03 04 — 10 9 8 7 6 5 4 3 2 1

Library of Congress Cataloging-in-Publication Data

Dittes, James E.
    [When work goes sour]
    Men at work : life beyond the office / James E. Dittes.
       p.   cm.
    Originally published: When work goes sour.
  Philadelphia : Westminster Press, © 1987.
    ISBN 0-664-25481-0 (alk. paper)
    1. Work (Theology) 2. Men—Religious life. I. Title.
  [BT738.5.D58   1996]
  248.8'42—dc20   96-21398

Men at Work

Contents

Preface

Men's most intense love affairs are often with work. As with other love affairs, the experience is sometimes joyous, sometimes devastatingly disappointing. As in other love affairs, we often expect a fulfillment never attained. As in other love affairs, we often discover our ardor unrequited or our commitment one-sided. Probably the disappointment is greater in love affairs with work than in love affairs with people, because work is not really a very good love partner.

Men's most intense religious commitment is often to work. We give it absolute devotion, and we expect our work to save us, to make us feel whole and healthy and right, cured from the gnawing sense that there is something wrong with us. Sometimes it does this, for a while. But often the sacramental powers of work become crumbled idols, and we find ourselves religiously dedicated to a god unworthy of our ardor, trusting a god unable to deliver a saving.

Let us keep love for people, religious hope and commitment for God, and let work be work: no more, no less. We probably do our work better when we don't take it so seriously (see chapters 4 and 5), even though we do need to take seriously the pain we feel (see chapter 1) when we do, inevitably, take work very seriously indeed (see chapter 2).

More important, let men be men, not workers. Let us recognize that we can and do stand tall, hearty, worthwhile without work; we don't need work to prop us upright. It is painful to strip the workaholic of his drug, but that's one way of discovering that he *is* truly a man, a man of stature and esteem, without it. Love and God are both available to us without *working* for them.

Women in our day have discovered that often their drug has been dependence on men, and that this dependence has left them vulnerable to battering and oppression. The cure for the battering and oppression is in giving up the dependence, not in giving up the men. For men, the cure for the battering and oppression meted out by their work is in giving up the dependence on that work, not in giving up the work. We don't *need* work to be whole, fulfilled human beings—there has been too much exaggerated sentiment sold us (as too much romanticism has been sold women) about the fulfilling meaning of work. We work because it has *some* meaning, *some* interest, accomplishes *some*thing, and because it pays us.

This book is about *men's* love affairs with and religious commitments to their work and about getting unhooked from such dependencies. If women readers see something familiar about themselves in these patterns, that is for them to say. While I am writing this book, I imagine myself sitting among a group of men, unburdening myself of some of these experiences and reflections for the first time. I revel in the idea of men getting together and leveling with each other, dropping the charade of Impassive Successful Worker, admitting the pain of work, and discovering, maybe for the first time, how much there is to life and to me, to each of us—once we peel off the worker role.

Preface to the Second Edition

Ten years ago, this book proposed to track how it is that we men make a religion out of our work: We give work our ultimate devotion and, in exchange, expect our work to bestow a blessing, to feed our souls. Since our work turns out to fail this assignment, since our fervent devotion to it leaves our souls all the more hungry, our work proves a false religion, an idol not God. The book, as I read it then, focused on this falseness. I gave it a title that emphasized the failure (*When Work Goes Sour*). I presumed to take a "prophetic" posture against this false religion. I mildly scolded men (even while also wanting to be pastorally sympathetic with their frustrations) for pursuing this false god. And I came out in favor of trusting our souls and our lives to God instead of to our work.

A decade later, this is still the plight of most men I know—although we are now more excruciatingly aware of how doubly maiming to the soul it is to put religious trust in work when you don't have any work. A decade later it is still urgent advice: Let your work be just work, let God be your God, so as to stand a better chance of letting a man feel like a man. I still aspire, someday, to be able to heed the advice myself.

But I find something else in the book when I read it now, an element of realism that is also an element of hope, something in men to be admired and trusted. It is this: If we men do make a religion of our work, let us give full appreciation to our talent and our desire, disclosed therein, for being religious.[1] Work may be an unworthy god, but the religious impulse is not unworthy. Among the forms of our work–religion the book mentions our capacity for ritualizing, for mysticism, for monastic renunciation, as well as our capacity for trust and commitment and loyalty to a call. In other words, our relationship to work does not just stifle our spirituality; it also discloses spiritual strengths that need to be commended, owned, and developed. The way from a work–religion to a truer religion is not by rejecting the work–religion for its falsity, but by developing its germs of faith.

JAMES E. DITTES

---

[1] I was led to this new reading of the book by reading my more recent attempt to probe men's religiosity, *Driven by Hope: Men and Meaning.*

Introduction:
Six Men

Let us take time to get acquainted with several men,
welcome them to our discussion, hear them begin
to tell about themselves, and invite them to stay
around and tell more of their stories from time to
time, as we proceed. These are not actual men—at
least the first four aren't—in the sense of identifi-
able individuals with names, addresses, and phone
numbers; they exist only in these pages. Neverthe-
less, they *are* composites of real men, with real
stories to tell of real experiences, real pain, real
moments of liberation; they exist all around us and
in our own lives. As these men tell their stories in
the chapters that follow, maybe you will see yourself
and want to say, "Me too." Even better, maybe these
stories will prompt you to say, "In my case what was
going on was like that, but . . . " Or, "It isn't like
that at all with me. What happens to me is . . . " Maybe
you'll tell your story to yourself, maybe to others.

In the pages of this book, we are trying to find ways
of understanding the experience of these men—and
your experience, and mine—and also to suggest ways
of changing that experience, where it could use some
changing. So the book may not mean much unless
we can get well acquainted with these men—and
with ourselves. I hope that can happen.

We men don't have much practice in sharing

important and troubled parts of our lives. We have been taught for a long time that it is risky to make yourself too vulnerable to another man. It is giving power to another to let him know something about you, especially where it hurts; in the competitive world of men against men, we should never yield power to another. Maybe this is one way "work" has taken over our lives; we make our relationships, with other men and even with ourselves, too much like the world of work, where life is competitive, even cutthroat, and everything is measured in terms of success or failure, achievement or defeat.

Maybe there are other ways, "nonworking" ways, trusting ways, in which we can think about ourselves and talk about ourselves, even with other men. So listen to these men—they aren't used to revealing themselves, either—and listen to the men around you, if you get a chance; maybe even disclose something of yourself.

I do not want, if I can help it, to make *work* out of this book. What is most important to me is not whether I can manage to say things that are brilliant or gripping or best-selling. This book is not an end in itself. Its importance is whatever it prompts *you* to say—to yourself or to others. Put the book aside, whenever the time is right, and think about it or start talking about it with someone. The important thing is not my words but your experience—or, even more important, *our* experience.

To begin to discover and share our own experiences, let us listen first to Paul and Andy and the others.

PAUL

Paul had worked hard to make the Saturday afternoon kite-flying time with his eight-year-old son Ronnie a fun time, a close time, a real father-and-son time of the kind he knew they both wanted and hadn't had much of. But when it was all over, it felt flat, like a stale root beer, as though they had gone through all the right motions but nothing had happened. Paul felt drained and tense—he went to the den and collapsed with a beer in front of the TV. Ronnie had just stood around, bored or distracted, and at the first chance, when his father said, "Let's quit," he dashed off down the street to find Ken. It was a big disappointment for Paul, and he felt cheated as he sat there looking at the beer can with the TV blaring, cheated, maybe puzzled, maybe a little angry. High hopes, to which he had given his best, and nothing had happened—something like the way lovemaking with Mary seemed to end up all too often lately. Sometimes he felt like this at the end of a day's work, too, but he called that "burn-out," and with Ronnie it just seemed like nothing had even started.

He knew he had not been finding enough time or making enough effort to get close to Ronnie. That's why he had cleared everything for this Saturday afternoon time, and asked Ronnie what he most wanted to do. "Oh, nothing special," Ronnie had said. "You got excited about those kites we saw the kids flying last weekend," Paul insisted. "Yeah, OK, sure . . . "—that's the way Ronnie had been all afternoon. Paul was paddling upstream, working hard and not getting anywhere. They went to pick out a kite: "Here's a good sturdy one. You like the colors?" "Yeah . . . sure. . . . " "How much string do you think we need?. . . . I bet it's going to fly really high." "Oh . . . I dunno. . . . "

They laid the kite out on the ground. "Let's fit the ends of these sticks into the pockets . . . no, not that way, like this." "Dad, look at Skipper chasing that squirrel." "I'll bet Skipper is going to want to chase this kite. . . . Why don't you try putting that stick in the pocket over there." Upstream—hard work—and getting nowhere.

Laboriously assembled, the kite was finally ready
to fly. "Now, we're going to have fun. . . . I'll get it
started up in the air and then you can fly it. . . . Why
don't you sort of toss it up in the air when I tell
you? . . . No! Not yet!"

And after it was up: "Doesn't that look neat up
there in the sun? Here, you take the string. When
the kite starts to go down, just pull the string, and
when the kite wants to go up, let the string out. You
think you've got that? What did I just say now?"

Finally the kite was down and both were released
to go off their separate ways. Paul felt drained and
depressed. He really had wanted to get close to his
son, and he had done everything he could. But it just
didn't happen. He didn't know what else to do. He
decided Ronnie didn't really want to get close to
him. Was this Ronnie's fault or had Mary been
somehow turning the boy against his father?

ANDY

Andy could be the model for a fashion magazine.
He is a handsome blond thirty-five-year-old with a
rugged face that's weathered as if from sailing. And
he's wearing the clothes of a sailor, jeans and a
dark-blue, coarsely knitted turtleneck sweater. But
it turns out his work is not out on deck but inside at
a desk, much to his disgruntlement. "I've always
loved the smell and the feel of wood." He is actually
caressing a polished wood key-chain tab while he
talks. "I just like to make things out of wood. But I
got too good at it, so I can't do that any more. I used
to work out of a basement, then out of my neighbor's garage. I'd make furniture, mostly built-in
desks for dens and cabinets for kitchens. But I
would get to standing around somebody's place and
make suggestions for redesigning the whole room:
'Build in benches there and move that window over
here,' and so on. I would think of the whole room

as one integrated piece of furniture. And I began doing bed headboards with lighting controls and stereo radio and all that. So the jobs got bigger and I got more of them. Pretty soon I had to hire a helper, and then a lot more, and we had to move out of George's garage and I had to build my own building. Then I got in over my head on designing these rooms and had to take on an architect, then somebody to sit in the office and handle the payroll and the billing and everything. So now I spend all my time at a desk, estimating jobs and looking over architects' drawings and interviewing people to hire and studying magazines and manufacturer's catalogs, or going to conventions to keep up on new ideas in design and materials. I wish I could get back out there and just polish wood all afternoon, or else spend the afternoon in a kitchen while some woman tells me how a desk over in a corner under the stairs will save her life and everything she wants the desk to be able to do for her."

I guess Andy's story could be the story of a surgeon or a teacher or an accountant, caught up in the machinery and routines and politics of the job, deflected by the success at work from the meaning of the work: owned by the work, working for the work.

LEN

Len caught himself with both hands in midair, a paper in each hand, baffled for a split second as to which paper was to go into which out basket. "I've become a paper shuffler." It was the first time he had used these words about himself. He accepted the label with as much pride as amusement, and no disdain. Making these decisions, getting things going in the right direction, scribbling the right reply on a memo, deciding which of these things to take to a meeting and how to present them—he

had acquired all this paperwork with the new title
("Department Manager" is what it said on the door,
not "Paper Pusher"). All these things were important and made a difference. The paper felt good in
his hands, maybe like bricks to a mason laying up
a wall, one brick at a time. Every paper moved to
the out basket built the wall higher. Len made each
decision carefully, knowing that the messages he
sent along and the way he sent them would set
events in motion that would determine important
outcomes later on. The way he set each brick in
the wall would affect the rows to come. At the end
of the day, even at the end of an hour, he could
check off important tasks accomplished, decisions
made. What would they be saying ten years from
now?

Yet, in that split second with his hands poised,
uncertain whether the paper in his right hand moved
to the upper basket and the left to the lower, or vice
versa, there was doubt, a long enough pause for the
doubt to become fully formed in his mind, the doubt
that never came while his hands were busy and the
paper was moving. Does it really matter? What if I
put them in the wrong boxes? What if I send this
report back to the committee and move the other
one along, rather than vice versa? What if I had not
asked for those reports in the first place? What if I
had not invented the new committee structure? All
these bricks so painstakingly, even lovingly, put into
place one by one, each a firm accomplishment—
what if this is all private busywork, a tree crashing
in the forest and no one listening? When the history
of the world is written, or the history of this organization, or even the history of my own life, will
anyone admire these carefully laid bricks? Will anyone notice how straight and firmly laid they are?
Will there even be a wall?

The hands had to move on fast or they would not
move again, because inside him Len knew the

answers all too well. The hands moved on but the heart gradually withdrew to protect itself.

When Len thought of writing his first annual report, he knew he would work late at night and come up with a roster of accomplishments, and he knew other people would be checking off his report and moving the paper into their own baskets. But he also knew the report would be a world of its own without roots in any other world. More like the bluffing talk around the poker table, which might or might not bear any connection with the cards, and nobody knew or much cared. When Len goes to lunch with some of the same people he is exchanging paper with, they don't talk about any of these things he has put energy into all morning. When he tries to discuss this report or that memo or the agenda for a coming meeting, they brush it off—just as though it weren't important enough to talk about on real time. Most of them have been in their jobs a year or two longer than Len has.

So he goes back to his desk in the afternoon and pushes more paper. But those split-second moments of hesitation recur and get longer.

CLIFF

We catch Cliff shoveling snow, a lean and fit sixty-two-year-old. "No, this isn't my own walk—I finished that long ago. I always like to get my snow off before people tramp it down. This is the Johnsons' walk. Roger's already gone to work, I guess, and Martha must not be feeling very well. They'll certainly appreciate the help." Cliff was being very careful to get the walk entirely clean without damaging any of the grass alongside. He was also being careful, though it was a little harder, to throw the snow out toward the street and not back on the shrubbery. They would notice how careful he was being and really appreciate it.

Cliff had plenty of time to help his neighbors these days, thanks to Mr. Mersick. It was almost a month since Mr. Mersick had called him in to say that he had just worked his last day for the company. They thought Cliff might like to retire a couple of years early and not wait until he was sixty-five. So they were going to rearrange the Accounting Department to make that possible.

What was hardest to get used to was the idea that Mersick's could get along without him. On snowy days like this, he would always get up early to trudge to work, even when the buses weren't running. He had always stayed through supper on those busy days at the end of the month, because he knew they needed him. When they asked him to spend those two years taking the bus every day way over to the Westville branch he was happy to do that because he knew they needed him there, too. If only that had not been a bad year, he was sure they would have given him a good bonus.

When Mr. Mersick had called him in that day last month, Cliff had been a little surprised. Not at being retired suddenly without notice—somehow, if that's what the company needed, that was OK. He was surprised that Mr. Mersick didn't seem to know that he had never missed a day at work in the last twenty-eight years, or that he had developed the system of weekly accounting feedback to each of the departments and that only he knew how to operate it. Even if Mr. Mersick didn't seem worried about how that was being managed now, Cliff was. But he wasn't going to try to call over there again; they had cut the conversation short when he tried that last week.

But now he was really going to get the Johnsons' walk clean—maybe Martha was looking out the window now—and then he was going to surprise his own wife by getting a load of laundry done. He didn't know what he was going to do this afternoon.

AARON

Aaron is a middle-aged man, bearded, long-haired, with a weathered face. He is dressed in the garb of the Near East desert, from which he has just barely escaped with his life. The story is told in the book of Exodus, ending with chapter 32. Some of us may have heard his story before, how he was recruited, reluctantly, into assisting his brother Moses in leading the Hebrew people out of Egypt and through the wilderness toward the Promised Land, how he was left alone with the disgruntled and frightened people while Moses went off to Sinai, how he yielded to the people's pleas to construct a visible, tangible god, a golden bull, and how this act of idolatry infuriated Moses and God. His story may be ancient and legendary, but it also sounds very contemporary: dedicated commitment and the acceptance of responsibility going unappreciated, even disparaged.

Here's how Aaron might tell his story to us:

"I was just trying to do my job, meet my responsibilities—I could have turned my back and walked away, but I was being conscientious. I was just trying to do what they had taught me. But instead it made them furious. My brother Moses had got me into this business. He said I could do some things better than he could, like making speeches, and he needed me. So I went along and did everything I was told to do and did it well. That included some pretty strange stuff, like turning my walking stick into a snake, or holding it over the Nile to fill the river with blood or with frogs, or hitting the ground with it to turn the dust into gnats, or throwing ashes up into the air to turn into boils on the Egyptians [Ex. 7–9]. The idea seemed to be to improvise with whatever you had at hand, even if it seemed outlandish, and trust in God to make it work out OK. A lot of these things went against my own good sense and better judgment, but I was really trying hard to be a team player and do what they wanted.

"Then Moses abandoned me and the people. He went off to consult God—he used to take me with him but not any more—but that's a different issue. So there I was with the people, lost, frightened, angry, hungry, thirsty. They all looked at me and said, 'Do something, lead us out of this.' I could have shrugged my shoulders and said, 'Don't look at me. Moses got us into this, wait till he gets back.' But I really felt I owed it to these people and to Moses and to God to do something, the best I could. So I scratched my head and remembered my stick turning into a snake, which they said was a good sign. Then I noticed all the earrings people were still wearing and realized that maybe that was a mistake out here in the desert. That wasn't doing anybody any good, and it might be a responsible thing to give up these gaudy earrings and do something better with the gold. Another snake didn't seem right, so I worked hard to shape a beautiful animal out of all the gold. Do the best I could, get something that would stir people and make them rally together again, and then trust God to carry on from there— the way we had from the first plagues in Egypt—that was my idea. If Moses and God had been around to tell me what to do, I would have done it exactly. When they weren't around, I had to figure out what would be the best thing, what they would probably want.

"But it turned out, just trying to do my job well, I did something they didn't like. Moses was furious. He dropped the tablets he was carrying. He smashed the beautiful animal we had made, ground it up, and made the people drink the gold. Can you believe it? Drink it! What an emotional overreaction. I think he was probably jealous because I had gone ahead and done something without his advance approval. He always was that kind of brother. But I swear I wasn't trying to one-up him. I was only trying to do a good responsible job, exactly the job he got me into, and I just barely got away with my life. It's the end of the line as far as me and that whole project is concerned."

And, indeed, Aaron is not heard of again in the Bible.

JOSEPH

Joseph joins us also wearing the robes of the Near East. But his clothing is not worn and drab from years of nomadic wandering in the desert. His robes are laundered and decorated, his beard closely trimmed. Still a young man, he has gone all the way to the top in political and economic power. He manages the long-range economy for the region. Today he would be minister of oil. (You can read about his success and his difficulties in getting there in the last quarter of the book of Genesis or in almost any set of Sunday school lessons.) Grand success that he is, he wants to tell us that success does not come easy and that, above all, it leaves a lot to be desired.

"The kids used to call me 'teacher's pet' and they didn't like me much. I didn't have a lot of friends. I was pretty lonely, and still am. But it always seemed very important to me to be doing the right thing, to be conscientious, to be responsible, to be doing whatever job had to be done, and above all to be doing it honestly and doing it well. That doesn't always suit other people, and you get into trouble. But that's the way it is and has to be.

"I was close to my father, his favorite of all the boys and the one who tried hardest to do what he wanted and make things go right for him. When my brothers would be messing up in their work, I would usually come and tell him about it. Eventually they ganged up on me and roughed me up and even hired somebody to kidnap me. But whatever it costs, somebody has to stand up for what's right and do what is right.

"Another time I was really doing the responsible thing and it got me into a lot of trouble—it's not fair, but that's the way it happens. I had got a good job running the house for a rich man, Potiphar—some people, at least for a while, really appreciate somebody who knows how to do honest responsible work. But this guy's wife tried to seduce me, and of course I wouldn't go along with that stuff; I was loyal to my boss. I just walked out on her and told her where to get off. So she got furious with me and framed me and got me thrown in jail. If I had been willing to forget my responsibilities and play along with her, I would have saved myself a lot of trouble.

"But jail wasn't so bad. I didn't get along with the other guys there too well, but I got along fine with the jailer. He saw I was a clean, responsible guy and soon made me a trusty, really running the jail for him. That's sort of how I worked out the lucky break to get a chance to talk to the king.

"I told the king what he wanted to hear and gave him some good economic advice—I really do my homework and know what I'm talking about in a spot like that. So he gave me the job of running the economy, and that's where I am now. I made it to the top by the age of thirty. It's a lot of work and a lot of responsibility, but that's what I'm good at and that's what I like.

"Sure, there's not much else in my life. I don't see much of my wife or two sons. [They are barely mentioned in the otherwise long and detailed published accounts of Joseph's life, Gen. 41:50–52.] I don't have many friends. When my brothers showed up quite by surprise, I was much moved, but I couldn't let that get in the way of doing my official job. So I didn't even tell them who I am. I ducked out for a minute to let the emotions pass and to get hold of myself. Then I came back and dealt with them in a straight, official, responsible way. I told them they would have to follow certain rules, such as if they wanted to do business with me and get our help, they would all have to come and live here. Some people might think I'm not looking ahead and that I'm setting them up to be entrapped, maybe even enslaved, here in Egypt. But those are the rules.

"The last thing my father ever said about me was to call me 'one set apart from his brothers' [Gen. 49:26]. I call that a compliment. I don't pay much attention to the people who say that being 'set apart' is not a good way to live. Maybe they're right. My father also said about me, 'His enemies attack him fiercely and pursue him with their bows and arrows. But his bow remains steady, and his arms are made strong by the power of the mighty God' [Gen. 49:23–24]. 'When the going gets tough the tough get going,' I always say. It's tough trying to be responsible and do the right thing, so you have to be tough. That's what comes first. Tenderness, or vulnerability as they talk about it these days, or caring about people at the expense of caring about the job that has to be done—that kind of thing leads you astray. Yeah, I sure am someone who is 'set apart.' "

Now, is it time to hear from you? How is it with you and your work?

1

The Pain
of Work

We have just heard men in grief—Paul, Andy, Aaron—and we have also heard the seemingly more upbeat Cliff, Len, and Joseph covering their grief, but just barely, with head high and a set smile. Work leaves most men, I think, with an abiding and gnawing grief. Work has its joys, for some men some of the time, deep joy; the aim of this book is to restore that joy to our work. But first, let's be honest about the grief it brings.

My *work* can leave me in grief? you wonder. Grief is felt when someone dies, isn't it? Someone you care about, someone you have opened yourself up to and allowed to share your life in some way, someone you have come to count on for emotional connection and support—when that person dies, you feel some part of yourself is wrenched away, the rug pulled out from underneath you. You feel a little lost or confused, off balance. The world seems overwhelming for a while, and you feel small. You can't eat or sleep too well and you don't have much energy. You aren't much interested in people or even in your work. That's grief; it happens when someone dies—right?

Partly right. It happens other times too.

Sure, if there's a divorce, or maybe when the kids leave home or when a love affair breaks up, or you get sick for a long time. Some important part of your life is gone, some important part of yourself is lost or rejected, and you feel emptied, hollowed. Things get out of focus for a while, until you pick up the pieces and rebuild.

Or maybe even when you are out of work, when you retire, go on disability leave, or, of course, get fired. That's the same kind of loss and rejection, and you feel down for a while until you begin to get it together again. But how can you talk about "grief" *on* the job? As long as the work goes on, life goes on, and where is the grief?

Because work is full of disappointment and rejection. Men's love affairs with their work are as intense as their love affairs with any person, but it is an unrequited love. Men expect a lot from their work, and they don't get it. Men make a religion out of their work—"saving their souls" is not too strong a way to put it—but the religion fails.

Whatever sense of identity or fulfillment or contentment, whatever sense of place in the scheme of things, whatever esteem a man yearns for, he most often expects it to come from his work. He gives a lot to the work. He makes himself vulnerable, usually more vulnerable than to any person, more vulnerable than he realizes. He is at the mercy of the work to pay off, to give him what he yearns for, what he has earned by his effort. When the work reneges, betrays, and fails to deliver, there is nothing he can do—except grieve.

To grieve is to take two coffee cups from the cupboard in the morning, only to remember that your wife is dead or separated from you . . . and you have to put one cup back.

To grieve is to start joyfully into the gift shop, your eye attracted by the perfect gift in the window, only to remember that the child is dead . . . and to walk on down the street, heavily.

To grieve is to be delighted with the snapshot prints at the drugstore counter and to impulsively order duplicates to share with your mother, only to remember that she died six months previously . . . and to say to the clerk, "Never mind."

To grieve is to wake up on a brilliant sunny morning in spontaneous, unbidden anticipation of playing golf, only to be reminded instantly by your heavy limbs that you have had a stroke . . . and to close your eyes, now moist.

To grieve is to have your heart broken, to have your inner being yanked open and a piece clawed away, to have rare and precious passions left dangling and twisting, abandoned and rejected—all because of the irretrievable loss of someone to receive and return those passions, to give place and wholeness.

But, also, to grieve is to find work draining your passions, not replenishing or arousing passions, to find work betraying and rejecting the very best you have given.

To grieve is to pour out energy and imagination into a report that really does analyze expertly and makes brilliant constructive recommendations—all during the writing being aware of the recognition and approval that will be forthcoming and the revisions it will set in motion—only to have the report filed with a curt "Thanks. I wonder if you could get to work on this thing that just came to my desk" or else a forgetful "Oh, yes, I did ask you to look that over, didn't I?"

To grieve is to have the boss level with you about the report, "Those recommendations are great ideas, if this were only an ideal world. But they step on too many toes. And you can't ask Henry to give up his turf that way." To grieve is to respond simply, "Sure, George."

To grieve is to be the team player, because that is the right way to be, passing around the data and the engineering tips, only to discover that the bonuses and promotions go to the ones who hoarded the data, theirs and yours. To grieve is to grunt, "Congratulations."

To grieve is to have an especially interesting job come into the shop, a job you automatically route to a favorite young protégé, only to have the word come back that he has just quit and gone to work for a competitor . . . and to look up confused, saying, "Who can do this?"

To grieve is to spend all day, all week, all year, all career moving around words or dollars or pieces of machinery in your own particular way in your own particular part of the world on your own particular assignment, just as though it made a big difference to anyone how you did it . . . knowing deep in your heart that it doesn't.

To grieve is to invest three years of hard work and excited energy in law school, and maybe a lot more in the practice of law, all because this offers the best hope of making society a more just place for your fellow humans, only to conclude, very reluctantly, that your energies are in fact serving and nurturing a legal apparatus that is dehumanizing . . . and then to toss in your bed at night and wonder, "Is it too late to start again . . . but where?"

To grieve is to prowl around the piney-odor unfinished rooms of the new house made possible by your recent spectacular promotion, feeling deep dreamy contentment over the good living you can now share with your family in the years ahead and congratulating yourself for making that possible, only to wonder in a few years where the contentment and the good times and the family have gone. You can remember clambering around the house under construction, but not much any more, since you have not been in the house much and since you have been drained of energy when you have been there. . . . But when you look around the family room for someone to share these regrets with and plan a restart, there is no one there.

To grieve is to begin a new job, excited about the team you are joining, because it offers the chance for collaboration and mutuality in which your own efforts will be appreciated and built upon, to feed into larger results in ways that didn't seem to happen when you were working more as a loner in a faceless organization—only to discover before the year is out that a team needs more than adjacent offices and connecting lines on a table of organization . . . only to wonder, still a loner, who you can work *with*.

Grief, then, is the emotional debris of separation, alienation from some central, familiar, fervently desired piece of one's own life. This is what work does to us.

Separation *from* work produces wrenching grief for men, because work looms so huge in the emotional economy and is looked to as the principal source of selfhood and happiness. This is as true when the separation from work comes at the end of the day or the end of the week as it is when the separation comes as an abrupt termination or retirement. A man may very well experience this grief every day at 5 P.M., especially on Friday.

But the grief still more wrenching and more to be talked about in this book is not separation *from* work but separation *by* work, the separation that work produces from so many other crucial parts of life: separation from family and friends, from your own emotional life, from hobbies and relaxation and play and fulfillment, from a sense of personal wholeness, from the very sense of achievement that work is supposed to produce. Our work, which at first promises to connect us with ourselves and with satisfactions and with other people, grows and dominates and takes on a life of its own, like connecting tissue in a body becoming cancerous, until it

demands massive energies for itself. We don't seem
to notice this at first—that is part of the trick—but
when we do, the grief is deadly. It is as though we
are building a road to get somewhere, and we keep
building and building and building the road, layer
upon layer, until, before we know it, it has become
a huge wall, an obstacle barring our way and maybe
even our view of the goal. Work has gone sour.

Work goes sour, work makes grief, in two important ways. We go to work for two kinds of payoffs
that work seems to promise us, the "after-work"
payoffs—money, status, leisure—and the more intrinsic "on-the-job" payoffs—a sense of achievement, worth, recognition, partnership. Work comes
to renege on both promises; it cheats us of the fruits
of our work and it cheats us of the meaning of our
work. And it is hard to say which grief is more
painful.

The after-work payoffs are mostly the things that
money can buy—a comfortable family life, time to
parent, to learn and read, to play, to be a good
citizen in community activities, to serve the church,
or a host of other things. We all know the excruci-
ating pain of discovering that the work has drained
us so much that we do not have energy or goodwill
or even interest left over for the things we once said
were more important than the work. The means
have swallowed up the ends. We still *say* that these
other goals of life are more important than our
work. But, in fact, our behavior says loud and clear
that we have come to give the work itself the highest
priority, and this priority of work over life takes on
a life of its own and keeps growing, snowballing,
smothering the life some remnant longing in us still
yearns for. This discovery, when we face up to it, is
one kind of sour grief. A man discovers all too
readily and all too painfully that the work is taking
over. The work is not working for him. He is working for the work. It does not get him where he is

going after work, but leaves him stranded at work. Work turns out to be not so much the way to a richer life as what gets in the way of a richer life.

Even more painful and less well recognized than grief for after-work goals, the extrinsic payoffs, may be grief for the at-work, on-the-job goals, the intrinsic payoffs. Here, too, work that promises to lead to a richer life takes over and gets in the way of that richer life, sabotaging it. This is less easy to admit because it is more painful, more humiliating, a more sour form of grief. One can feel foolish, victimized for being caught in this trap. And no man wants to feel foolish or victimized. It means he has lost control over his destiny; he has lost manhood. But, admitted or not, the pain is deep and gnawing.

This book is mostly about this on-the-job grief, the disappointment of work itself going sour, the work to which we have committed so much energy, so much hope and trust, so much of our very selves. We need to acknowledge the grief, where it exists (this chapter); to discover, if we can, how we got into this situation (chapter 2); to notice what the grief does to us (chapter 3); and to find ways of liberation (final chapters). Mostly we will discover that we don't *need* work to make us feel good about ourselves; we can learn to go to work for what it is—work still has *an* importance—but not for the high promises we think work is making to do something for us, because it really isn't making those promises.

Men go to work with relish. Getting the first job and then the first promotion, after an impatient adolescence and apprenticeship, feels like walking through a door into the real world where we will find our true self. We may cross the threshold of marriage with some apprehension. But we usually go to *work* with relish. This is it. This is *me*. We give most of our time, the best of ourselves, to work because here is where we expect to discover and confirm ourselves, to find ourselves centered. We expect to feel ourselves doing things, making a difference to the world, a good difference, making it a better place. We expect to have our skills and wisdom needed, called for, mobilized, enhanced, recognized, appreciated. We expect to find ourselves challenged, engaged, stretched, enlarged to meet and best the challenges, triumphant, tested and found able, more able than we or others suspected. We expect to be joined, to be engaging fellow workers as well as the task, to feel part of a team that makes us feel enlarged, enhanced, congruent.

We go to work with these high hopes, hearing these promises as to what we will be and do and become, of how work will work for us. In the moments when these promises come true, there is exhilaration and celebration. When the promises fail and the hopes fade, there is grief.

What names do we put on this grief? What words do we use?

Images of Grief

Burned Out

"Burnout" is the name most often used these days. If you use that name about yourself, what does it feel like?

Like the shell of a house violently gutted? Most of us are not so overtly victimized.

Like a rocket that has successfully launched its payload into orbit and can now parachute gently back to earth, spent but triumphant? That is claiming more success than most of us can.

Most often, I suspect, we use burnout for the discovery, somewhere in middle age, that the fuse is no longer lighted. It was lighted early in life, and we saw the spark moving steadily toward the gigantic blast-off to come. But now the spark has gone out. We miss that and are usually trying, often with some frenzy, to get it relighted.

"I have to make myself get up every morning right at seven, or I might stay in bed all day," Cliff tells us. "I think I need somebody in the office to screen all these phone calls," says Len, who used to get charged up, energized, by juggling the phone, snapping decisions, and keeping himself immersed in a thousand details daily—a kind of energy that most of the time he still can put into pushing papers. Because Len also says, "Some days I wonder if I'm just going through the motions. I don't feel really connected. It feels flat. I feel flat, flat like a dead beer, flat like one of those two-dimensional cardboard figures they set up in the grocery store windows."

Aaron talks like that, too, when we get to know him better. "I threw the ornaments into the fire and out came this bull," he says toward the end of his story (Ex. 32:24b). I didn't really do anything; it's all happening to me. Just going through the motions—I'm not really there any more. "Sidelined," many of us feel.

"I don't know where the years went," is the way Paul puts it. "It always seemed that Ronnie and I were going to have a close relationship, and I tried to do everything right. But now if we're going to have any time together, I've got to schedule way ahead and I've got to make an effort to get Ronnie involved." The spark of spontaneity succumbs to the laboring of the relationship. The spark is burned out.

Or, maybe, burned out means we feel like the gray, flaky ashes we find in the fireplace the morning after a roaring fire there cheered and warmed us. The fuel is consumed—the gas tank is empty—and there just is no more. We feel stoked with a "nonrenewable energy source" like a fossil fuel, not like solar energy. Our gas tank started out full enough for the whole journey, but now it's empty, and there is no more. "I've done everything I can think of,"

Paul says, "to try to get close to Ronnie, and I've run out of ideas." "I couldn't stand one more commit-tee meeting," Cliff recalls. "They were boring and tedious, and I would almost fall asleep. I used to work over the agenda ahead of time real closely, and set my goals, and even get some speeches ready. No more, no way."

Burnout: the spark that once was there, the fuel—the energy—that once was there; it's gone. The action is somewhere else. We watch it, dimly, from the sidelines. The light is gone. One opposite of "light" is "dark." Another opposite of "light" is "heavy." Dark and heavy is how we feel.

Pushing a Stone Uphill

The ancient Greeks told the story of Sisyphus, a ruler of Corinth who was punished for his trickery by being required to roll a stone to the top of a hill—but every time it got near the top, it rolled back. "Sisyphean" now appears in the dictionary with the meaning of "endless, unavailing, as a task or labor." That's how Paul feels when trying so patiently, step by step, to get some response from Ronnie, some glimmer of relationship—endless and unavailing. That's how Cliff feels in his lifetime quest for the recognition and appreciation that still eludes him, the quest pursued by his careful labors, step by step up the hill. That's how Andy feels, trying to get his wood shop organized so that all the administrative work will be settled and behind him and he can get back to what he loves, crafting furniture. That's how Len feels, arranging his committees and charts and memoranda, building toward the goal he never reaches and which begins to seem more and more distant.

After Aaron built the idol, the golden bull, he still wasn't at the top of the hill. To make the idol more of a savior, he discovered he had to embellish the scene, set the idol on an altar, create a liturgy, order a feast day, endlessly trying to bolster and prop up this creation of his own hands, to make it into the saving figure, the god he needed and had promised. Joseph must have found something Sisyphean about his recurrent fate—every time he might think he was getting somewhere playing the responsible son, the responsible servant, the responsible bureaucrat, he got slapped down.

There is truth in the old Greek story that puts Sisyphus at work on the rock as punishment for his past trickery. When you or I find ourselves rolling rocks uphill, it often seems that we have got ourselves into this spot, have somehow outsmarted ourselves, been too clever for our own good, and this is the consequence. Len's own cleverness sought and won promotion to this desk job in which he is now endlessly pushing papers uphill. Cliff, trying to please neighbors or bosses, and Paul, trying to please Ronnie, take on an endless, escalating task. One gesture, shoveling the front walk or whatever, is never enough; there's the driveway, and the walk to the garage, and on and on, never done.

Aaron and Joseph were in some sense too clever for their own good. They put themselves out on a limb with their designing and scheming, well intentioned as it was, and they were stuck with the consequences of their own cleverness, becoming servants to the fruits of their own designing. And that is exactly how it was with Andy: a snowball somehow growing in size and becoming more threatening as it ran uphill.

Discounted

Discounted merchandise is priced at less than full value, less than original or normal or promised value: "We *say* it is worth this much, but actually we will dispose of it for less than that." A discounted loan

yields you less than the face value. A discounted
worker feels undervalued or, more accurately,
double-valued. First, there is the labeled value. This
is the high value put on you with words when you are
hired and when you are retired and at passing cere-
monial moments in between. The labeled value may
even be expressed in terms of a handsome paycheck.
But then there is the actual value, made very clear—
as though the printed value on the label were crossed
out and replaced with large red numbers—in the
way you are treated in daily circumstances. "To discount: to depreciate, as by leaving out of account; to
disregard," the dictionary says.

"Let's have lunch sometime." That's one of the
standard, ritualized ways the double message gets
said, the double message of depreciation in the guise
of appreciation. So is "I especially need you to go
to work on this project [this committee]." But don't
wait around for your efforts on this assignment to
be regarded at face value any longer than you wait
around for the lunch invitation. Somehow the people with the power to appreciate or depreciate, the
power really to employ and engage your work and
talents, never seem to be the ones who really know
and understand those talents. And vice versa: the
people who really do appreciate you don't seem to
be the ones who gained the power in the organization. So you feel sidelined, benched, separated,
alienated from the main action to which you could
contribute, want to contribute, what you have been
promised by the label.

Being discounted is a form of grief that strikes
close to the heart and is not easy to talk about. But
Len can tell us of one episode thirty years ago when
he was still new on the job. "I was doing bookkeeping then, and I noticed that some customers, when
they paid bills, were scribbling some complaints
about a particular piece of merchandise. It was just
that piece, and a lot of complaints, so I thought I

ought to pass on the warning that that product was not doing well. Next thing, I heard two of the engineers talking in the men's room. 'That guy is new here, and he's only in bookkeeping.' So I began to be more careful about giving my advice to people who might appreciate it—whoever they are. I just stick to doing my own work. There's plenty of that, and I can keep finding more. Incidentally, they finally had to withdraw that product."

What Cliff says sounds pretty poignant, but he says it chin up. "How come I always felt so lonely at work, if I was part of a team, like they said?" Aaron: "When things were going well, Moses was the hero. It was 'Aaron who?' When things go bad, then they notice me, and I am the bum." Andy, telling about being stuck at his desk and out of the shop, but speaking for most of us: "What I do best I never get a chance to do because someone's yelling 'Where's this?' or the phone is ringing or I get to feeling guilty for neglecting business."

"Ronnie *said* that he wanted to fly the kite and wanted me to put it together, but he just stood there with his hands in his pockets, chattering about all kinds of stuff." "I know," Joseph adds. "Potiphar *said* he wanted an honest servant."

"It's easy to let them make you feel like a little kid, belittled," Len adds, "as though they are the big boys, the big-leaguers, and you're not one of them. They say you are, but they only kind of tolerate you, with a pat on the head instead of a real clap on the back."

"Once I was sitting in a committee meeting," Cliff recalls, "and just after I described how I'd been on this committee for the last two years and what we had been doing, the boss looked around—and I swear he looked right through me, as though I wasn't there—and said something like, 'Well, we're all starting out together fresh, so let's see where we can begin.' "

Used

Which meaning of "used" conveys the grief? "Used" meaning no longer new, secondhand, pre-owned, worn-out, depleted and ready for a rummage sale or an old-car auction? Or: "used" meaning manipulated, exploited, controlled by and for someone else's best interest? Or are these two forms of grief really one? Is there something about being exploited that is particularly wearying and wearing? I think so. So does Andy: "I don't care how hard it is wrestling the tools, if I'm doing what I want, I stay fresh all day. I don't even notice the clock, and I never get hungry or I just go out and drop money in the candy machine. But if I'm wrestling these papers, they can get me pinned to the mat and pooped." This reminds Cliff: "If I go with my wife to a museum, I get a lot more tired standing around watching her watch things than if I just take off and hike around the block." "Somebody told me the other day," Len remembers, "that my arms looked like they were on puppet strings, signing papers and moving them from the in basket to the out basket. I would rather have them say my arms looked like a symphony conductor's, but I guess I'm really following the beat, not giving it. It's probably fighting those strings and keeping them from getting all tangled up that gets me all worn out every day."

A man expects his work to be the main arena in which he will exercise some power, have some control. When he finds he is, instead, being controlled, something important to his manhood feels violated, depleted. The experience must help a man understand how a woman feels when raped. Only the man's experience is much milder—or is it? Something absolutely fundamental to his own sense of manhood—that indefinable sense of having initiative and control over his own destiny and the destiny of others—is preempted, commanded by others without his choice, and of course he feels depleted, limp, drained, used up, abused, owned, used.

How must an athlete feel after he takes a bribe to throw a game? Everything in himself that he has most valued is for hire, sold out to another's whim. The hollow loss of grief. He no longer has the capacity to play well, even if he willed it.

"I wonder," Paul muses to himself, "whether that has something to do with why I got so tired trying to get the kite put together and up in the air. I thought I was frustrated and worn out from trying to get Ronnie to respond. Maybe, instead of terrorizing him, I was letting him terrorize me and making myself—not too successfully—fit what I thought he wanted. That never really worked."

Drugged

Workaholic is a common label people pin on themselves these days and on each other. What does it mean to think of work as a *drug*, a "controlled substance"? What does it mean to think of yourself as *addicted* to work? Alcoholism is a painful, distressing disease; can we describe work in those terms?

If people call you workaholic, they usually mean you just can't leave work alone, like an alcoholic can't pass up a bar or a bottle. You can't pass a task without doing it, like Cliff doing the neighbors' walk, every piece of snow on it, or Len not being able to let a single piece of paper lie in the in basket overnight. You work all day, all evening, and all weekend and still feel anxious, if you take time off for church or a movie, about the work that is overdue and undone. You turn any situation into a job to be done, as Paul converted parenting into work. Life is a work binge, and you can't shake it off. Work is your master, not the other way around.

But there is more to workaholism than being hooked on a habit. Like alcohol, work numbs even

while it offers the illusion of vitality. You can drown
yourself in work, leave behind and escape from
whatever disappointments or dilemmas or tensions
lurk in your life. Stress can be avoided for a lifetime
by keeping at work—that's one reason the end of
work can be so catastrophic, whether on the weekend or at the age of sixty-five when you come face-
to-face with yourself. This is as true for job-produced
stress as for stress at home; you can turn your back
on either one by more work. Even the heavy feeling
of being numbed, routinized, automated, dehuman-
ized—the morning after—can be swallowed up by
another dose of work. Like a steady drinker, you
never need to notice that the vitality you feel while
under the influence is plastic, synthetic. Paul's enthusiasm when building the kite and "having fun
with Ronnie"; the turn-on Len gets from pushing
paper; Cliff and Joseph, with their relentless habit
of doing good deeds: these habits may be contrived,
artificial, routinized, disconnected—that is, just as
separated and sidelined as any grief. But in the
doing, we *feel* authentic and engaged, congruent. In
the doing, Paul really thinks he is having fun, Cliff
really thinks he is pleasing the Johnsons, Len really
thinks he is influencing management. They are at
work, and work works, doesn't it?

But work doesn't work, even while we especially
need it to. That is the main thing to learn about
workaholism. It is not just a habit we cannot shake.
It is not just a numbing, illusory escape. It is a
devastating tease. That is why, as with any other
drug, we keep needing a new fix. The fix we count
on, the fix we need so badly, doesn't really fix at all.

Work is like a slot machine. The signs in the
casinos say there is a payoff, and you hear the jangle
of quarters elsewhere in the room. But somehow it
is just because your machine does not pay off that
you keep feeding it quarters and laboring the handle. Monkeys easily learn to pull levers on banana-

dispensing machines. After the bananas give out, the monkeys will stay at work pulling the levers. But not too long—being intelligent creatures, they will quit, long before the age of sixty-five. If we do want to keep the monkeys at work for a very long time, we will turn the banana-dispensing machine into a tease—as the psychologists call it in their own bland working terms, we will provide "partial reinforcement." Others might call it "seduction." We will rig the dispenser to give out a banana every now and then, or maybe display pictures of bananas, or give out plastic bananas. Or we may propagandize the monkeys with signs all around promising bananas, or perhaps older monkeys will oblige us by helping with the tease: Too exclusively hooked on bananas ever to notice that their habit hasn't worked, indeed, all the more belligerently defensive about the habit because it doesn't work—this is what psychologists call "cognitive dissonance"—they will preach faith in bananas.

Work lures us and fixes us with this same seductive tease. The daily job, the lifetime career, seems to promise to welcome you, to give you a place, a chance to make a difference and to be effective, to be in the center of the action, to be a vital and important person connected with others. So too with working as a life-style, as a way of living, as a way of loving and parenting and playing and worshiping; working at being father, husband, citizen seems to provide the way to a guaranteed welcome among family and friends, to make a difference and be effective in these relationships, to be in the center of the action, to be a vital and important person connected with others. Doing becomes the way to be. Doing a job, doing it well, doing good, performing, managing and maneuvering, analyzing and solving, working—that's the good life, the way to contentment. This is the wisdom we have accepted, largely unexamined, and pass on to each other, passing it on more fervently when we have doubts. This is the life we have committed ourselves to, so it must be right.

Work does come through with its moments of payoff, the hints and memories and imaginings of contentment and satisfaction, the Boy Scout merit badges we accumulated, the retirement tributes we are earning. Joseph remembers the fine coat his father gave him for being a good worker and therefore a favorite son. Aaron remembers the acclaim and thrill when he produced a snake from his staff. "Ronnie really got into pitching the ball to me when I organized a game of catch last month," Paul remembers wistfully. Len has a bounce in his step when he leaves his desk clean and the morning's agenda all checked off. But these payoffs and good feelings don't quite reach the heart and don't last. The hints and the memories are filtered through the fog of disappointments and misses and—in the manner of addictions—their seductive lure is thereby enhanced.

So work traps and addicts, like alcohol, by teasing. It seduces by promising *and* disappointing. Or, perhaps better than alcohol, we should think about the analogy of sex. We now understand how our culture, abetting our own fantasies and wishes, holds out high promises for sex, promises so high they are sure to be disappointed, promises so high they are sure to keep us responding to disappointment with renewed trying, over and over again. Something lodged deep inside us by our own yearning and by the insistent indoctrination of our culture can propel us after the ecstasy which sex promises and gives us a momentary glimpse of but never sustains. Our addiction compels us to suppose the disappointment is only momentary and remediable and to suppose the fulfillment is the reality to be pursued and pursued again.

Most of us, except when we are fully caught in the

addiction, can see through the tease of alcohol and of sex for the illusion that it is—the emperor has no clothes—and we can turn our backs to it when we have to. We can learn to take alcohol and sex as part of our lives, frequently very good parts, but only parts, not as the very substance or savior of our lives. Workaholics have trouble getting that perspective on work.

Probably more men are addicted to the teasing drug of work than to alcohol or sex. Something lodged deep in us urgently wants it to be so, what our culture wants us to believe: devotion to work guarantees well-being, and any failure in this promised contract is a temporary aberration that can be overcome—by more work. Generals pouring more weapons and men into a failing war, just because it is failing and they are hooked. Physicians pouring more medicine into the body to overcome the side effects of the last medicine. Lawyers patching up loopholes and engineers patching up cracks by more of the intricate designing that produced them in the first place. A failing President covering up past lies with new lies. When we are not caught in it, it is easy to perceive and repent of the addiction and the desperate illusory hope that sustains it.

Many of us may still be too caught up in the devotion to work to sense that devotion as addiction. The alcoholic or sexaholic may need a cure, relief from his drug, but when *work* is the problem, real men will stay at work and get their jobs done and hold a straight course. Solid work will keep one steady and well off; work will keep life solid.

That's how addicts talk.

Work Idolized

"I'm giving a lot more than I'm getting" or "It's all giving and no getting." At bottom, that may be the most acutely painful way a man feels the grief over his work. All the loneliness, the sense of being abused, discounted, sidelined, treadmilled, leashed, starved—it all may be summed up in "It's all giving and no getting." One way of understanding this is to understand work as an idol.

What is an idol? An idol is something that is not God but which is treated as though it were God. "Treated like God" means two things: We expect a lot from it, and we give a lot to it. We expect more from an idol than it can possibly deliver because we expect from it what only God can deliver. We give an idol far more than it deserves, because we give it the loyalty and service and trust that only God deserves. We make an idol out of our work.

Sometimes we feel this way—all giving and no getting—about our marriage or parenting or our holidays or our church life. That usually happens when we make work, and idols, out of these parts of our life.

Aaron made an idol out of golden earrings. He crafted a golden bull. The people said the bull had delivered them from their bondage in Egypt and expected the bull to save them from their present misery. They gave the bull trust and worship with sacrifice and feasting, for them the ultimate in giving, even abandoning themselves. This made God mad, to be supplanted by an idol, and Moses on God's behalf. But God didn't really need to punish Aaron and the people; idols are always self-defeating, and idol trusters always disappointed.

The Bible story seems to want to tell us that idol-making people are villains, offending God. But behind that is the lesson that idol-making people are victims. Self-punishment, pain, and grief are built into idol worship. Giving more than the idol knows how to receive, expecting far more than the idol can deliver—that is pain enough. The golden bull did not respond to their worship, did not receive their sacrifices, did not grant their prayers. So, as idol

worshipers are wont, addicts all, they redoubled
their giving into a frenzy, into an orgy ("the people
sat down to a feast which turned into an orgy of
drinking and sex" Ex. 32:6b). In their lostness and
hunger in the wilderness, they needed a God badly
("make us a god to lead us" Ex. 32:1). It was their
need that set them up to expect a lot and to give a
lot, and to be disappointed in their expectations and
drained in their giving.

They *needed* a God. They needed a *God*. They
needed to be saved from their deepest distress, and
for this they needed a power, as we often say, greater
than themselves. So it is with us and the idol we call
work. When you make an idol, you dare not admit
you are making an idol. You must believe it is a god,
and you must believe it has power over you, saving
power, not the other way around. "I threw the ornaments into the fire and out came this bull" (Ex.
32:24b), Aaron shrugged, denying his own hand in
the creation. Out of our need that the god will serve
and save us, we need to serve and save the idol. Save
it especially from any hint of failure or weakness,
especially from any hint that it is of our creation and
therefore not a "power greater than ourselves." We
exalt and defend it. We bow and submit to it. We
deny any choice or responsibility or power over its
place in our life. We become its creature, the bar-
gain we think we need to make to guarantee its
saving of us. We accept whatever pain it brings,
whatever abuse, whatever disappointment, just as
quietly as apparently the Hebrew people swallowed
the ground-up debris of their golden bull. So we
create, exalt, trust, submit to, and suffer from the
idols we treat as gods.

For those of us who have made work our savior,
it is easy to see how *others* are trapped in the vain
worship of idols of *their* making: sex, children, parents, political leaders, jogging, golf. But the true
believer never questions his own blind faith, espe-

cially when there are any hints that he may be blind to the limited powers of his god/idol. So our work is not an idol, it really is our savior.

Is it any wonder we feel so alienated from the work—so distanced, so out of focus, so out of tune with it—when we have such a need to disguise and pretend, to disguise our true history with it, the history of our compact with it, the history of our setting it up as the savior to be served, our need to pretend that it is something it is not?

"What else is there?" Paul and Cliff and Len shrug when we ask them whether they may have exaggerated the importance of work and working. For them it is a given, not a choice. That *is* the way to build a kite, to play with your son, to be a neighbor on a snowy morning, to get through a workday of decisions and memoranda and meetings. That *is* the way to be somebody, to have a clear conscience, to feel right about yourself, to get others to feel right about you: to give conscious effort and energy to solving problems and arranging things and accomplishing and achieving, to doing well and doing good. Keep doing until the payoff of good feelings comes, well, keep doing it until maybe the payoff comes. Well, keep doing it. . . .

. . . cheated, giving a lot and getting not much.

Mostly, Paul and Cliff and Len don't say much. They sit there quietly. There isn't much to say when the conversation begins to review lifelong unquestioned commitments.

2
Falling in Love with Work

Why do men—when we do—overcommit to work? Why do we go about work and working so intently, so compulsively, so insistently, so exclusively, so trustingly—far beyond what's good for us? Why do we become so infatuated, so enamored of work, in a love affair that is so one-sided and unrequited? Why do we work so religiously?

I think it is because we all need to turn to something to rescue us from what feels most fundamentally wrong with ourselves. Some of us, some of the time, search for the perfect woman to make our life seem more whole. Some turn to our children to complete us. Some may still turn to religion. But these days most of us men, most of the time, turn to our *work* to save us, to make us feel our life is living up to what it should be. Even when we turn to another person, or to marriage, or to children, or even God, we *work* at these relationships. We turn to work on the job; we turn to working as a style of life, as the way to live, as *the* way to make ourselves feel alive. Working becomes the sacrament that will restore us when we are feeling down, incomplete, somehow in the shadows and only an approximation of what we should be. Work will put us back on track, make us feel fully ourselves again—or at last. Work becomes our religion.

Work gives us a set of rituals to perform, things we can *do* to give us the sense that we are managing and assuring our own destiny and, indeed, influencing forces larger than ourselves. This will be discussed later in this chapter as "The Ritualizing of Work." Work also makes us feel that we belong to and blend with the larger controlling powers of life, that we are embraced and sustained by them. This will be discussed later in this chapter as "The Mysticism of Work." And there is a third way that work may be religious: work concentrates our attention and dedicates our energies in selected arenas that receive absolutely top priority while we withdraw from other arenas of life. This will be discussed as "Work as Monasticism."

We seem to be burdened with a deeply gnawing, unquenchable doubt about our own worth, status, place, destiny. "Am I all here?" we wonder about ourselves. We feel wrong or partial or broken or missing or sick, and we want to feel whole and healthy.

I know these feelings are not very close to the surface. You and I have spent a lot of energy trying to quell and salve these feelings. Especially we are not about to admit to each other that we have them. But the feelings still haunt us, maybe in tossing during the night, maybe in the quiet clutch we feel in our gut when we hear of someone our own age dying.

Maybe it has something to do with being expelled at birth from a comfortable, carefree haven into a cold, alien world in which we just don't fit so effortlessly. Maybe it has something to do with spending so many important years as little kids in a world run by big people. Maybe, for boys, it has something to do with the childhood discovery that we are different from the parent closest to us, our mother; and however many years and however much energy we spend protecting and celebrating that difference, learning to be macho, it still may seem, somehow, a difference not in our favor. Maybe for us it has something to do with regarding one's own penis as small and limp, deficient when compared with the prevailing notion that a real man's penis is big and hard and busy most of the time. Maybe it has something to do with what theologians called "original sin" or what psychologists call "existential anxiety," the conviction that there is something fundamentally and unavoidably disrupted about the human condition. Maybe it has something to do with the fantasy, made very vivid by our Calvinist ancestors, that our proper and natural destiny is eternal torment in hell, unless we are lucky or clever enough to have something special intervene to save us. (Something special like our own good work?) Maybe it has something to do with the prevailing imagery in the Bible describing how it is with people, especially God's people: evicted from the garden, sent out like Abraham on unknown journeys, held in captivity and in exile, wandering in a wilderness seeking a homeland, even, once in the homeland, still constantly straying from high calling and national destiny. Maybe it has to do with hearing of a Christ who is a social misfit and outcast, and a young church constantly at odds with itself and with the society around it—all vivid and resounding portrayals of how it feels to be out of step with one's self.

"I've always felt so helpless around Ronnie," Paul reports. "Ever since he was born, I've never quite known how to handle him, like I wasn't really his father or something." "I can feel Ronnie's side of that," Andy replies. "I always felt I must have been an adopted orphan, not really a full member of my family." Len says, "I don't know about 'anxious'— that may be too strong. I know I feel tense, uncomfortable, waiting for something to happen, unsettled, mentally pacing the floor, when I'm not working. Sitting at my desk really calms me down."

The Ritualizing of Work

The best defense, or at least the quickest defense, seems to be a good offense. If something is awry, if something is askew, *do* something. Attack the problem, or at least attack something, somehow. Name it, know it, analyze it, solve it, master it, control it, overpower it, do something. Work at it. Work it over. Work is the antidote to vulnerability, and therefore a man's first recourse.

A man falls sick, he starts to itemize the symptoms, put a label on the disease, analyze its causes, prescribe the cures, boss his nurses, chart his recovery, and explain it all. Keep well, keep control, keep himself by keeping at work.

A vacation looms, maybe as distressing as a disease because it also throws the man into a kind of unfamiliar wilderness. So he reacts in the same way, takes charge of it, works at it.

A couple may feel uneasy as their plane jolts down through cloud cover on the way to a landing—a vivid moment of feeling out of one's element, on the edges of usual experience. She may say "That's scary" or "Hold my hand," but he is more likely to explain clouds and aerodynamics; that is, more likely to go to work.

When lost in a strange part of the city, the woman will plead, "Let's ask directions." The man will insist on finding his own way, on working out his own solution.

The famous Protestant work ethic seems to have come about just this way: Calvinists, made anxious about whether they would be plucked from hellfire, because such "election" was thought to be arbitrarily irrational (an appropriately economic view of salvation in which the desirable goods were thought to be scarce), did what they could: they worked. As their work prospered, they found it natural to decide that their own prosperity in this world was a good sign, maybe even a guarantee, of God's favor and of heaven to come.

Whether we want to call it magic or superstition or legalistic religion or Protestant work ethic, this fundamental formula is lodged so deeply in us, prerational, nonrational, as to be a genuinely religious conviction! The deepest sense of wrongness and vulnerability about us can be quelled by work. Swinging the hammer, adding up the numbers, putting words on paper, running the meeting, working down the checklist one by one, solving the problem—it feels better; *I* feel better. Call it therapy, magic, religion—it may not be much different from any other primitive tribal ritual dance warding off evil spirits.

It must start early, this recourse to the ritual of work, this sense among boys that if only I *do* something, danger will pass me by and I will be well. A girl feeling troubled may most naturally reach out to her mother for cuddling; for a boy that sometimes seems dangerous. He may have a sense that as a male he is different from his mother and needs to protect his maleness by keeping his distance, alone. This is a big source of male self-reliance and independence, challenging the world on his own. The boy may also be left on his own more if his mother feels the same need to protect this difference; she can bond with her daughter more intimately but needs to see her son standing separately on his own two feet, someone she cannot so much bond with as admire. Especially is a boy urged on his own, urged to work in the world, by parents and everyone else, in a culture that defines maleness—and each male—as self-reliant, performing, working. "Jump up, you're a big boy . . . you can do it . . . figure it out for yourself . . . show 'em what you've got . . . take a cut at it . . . go, go, go . . . chores before play . . . homework before TV . . . practice . . . perform . . . work." Mastery is expected—not very long ago,

boys were *called* "master." "Why" is encouraged
and answered, figuring things out, exploring, explaining, dominating, relating to your world actively, not passively. That's work.

Few of us remember much about those early days
when we got started in the ways that seem such a
fixed and natural part of ourselves now. But Cliff
remembers this: "My father would always get impatient if I lagged behind when we were hiking. 'We'll
rest when we get to the end and not before,' he
would say, that and 'Everybody carry your own
pack.' I would usually make it to the end, though he
never much liked the way I came dragging in."
(Somebody listening might wonder if part of Cliff
wonders how upset his father would be about his
not still working at Mersick's right up to the age of
sixty-eight.) "My father didn't want me to ask *why*,"
Len remembers. "At least not ask him. Every time I
asked that, he would tell me I had to go figure it out
for myself and then come and tell him." These do
sound like work assignments. "That's why I wanted
to help Ronnie," Paul protests in response to Len.
"I just didn't want to leave him on his own. Don't
pass up anybody who needs some help, they always
said, the good Samaritan and all that. 'If somebody
needs your help, it's your job to help.' " (Your *job?*
somebody might observe.)

Are we talking about "macho"? These quotes may
sound a lot like the usual understanding of machismo: a man feeling insecure, his manhood threatened, overcompensates dramatically by asserting
himself in a highly exaggerated way, often through
violence or sex and almost always in the form of
demeaning and manipulating others. Well, of course
we are not talking about machismo that blatant,
though we may have to ask the question again in the
next chapter when we consider some of the ways we
respond to the griefs of work. We don't want to
argue that work is hurtful to others—except in those

times when we work on others or work them over. Our main concern in this discussion is understanding how and why and whether work is hurtful to us, the workers.

Working is a kind of machismo, a way in which we do set out to construct, with our own bare hands, some sense of presence or selfhood or competence when and because we have some doubts about those things. I just feel more comfortable, more of a somebody, more like I am all here, when I am working— moving things, making things, figuring things out, solving problems: the rituals of work, the self-constructing, identity-enhancing function of work.

The Mysticism of Work

There may be another way in which we work "religiously." We've just talked about work as a kind of ritual way of giving ourselves a sense of contact, control, presence, assurance. There also may be *mysticism* in our working. If the ritual is a way by which working expresses our macho side, perhaps the mysticism is what working does for our feminine side.

A mystic aspires to a direct, immediate connection with the mysterious powers that govern and sustain life. Not control or manipulation of the powers—that is the ritual function of work just discussed—but connection with those powers. Traditional mystics report their experience in religious terms: direct encounter with God during prayer, for example. But there are other common ways that people say they come to feel this contact with what is most real, most ultimate, most mysterious about life. Whether on a mountaintop or at sea, whether at sunset or at moonrise, whether in sexual orgasm or from drugs, the experience is a connection with whatever is whole and important about your life. You feel absorbed, enveloped, sharing embrace with, rooted, home. You feel a *thereness;* you feel "all there" by being connected to what is most "all there."

It's the opposite of feeling sidelined or hijacked or alienated, shunned or spurned, partial—the alienation and grief that work all too often actually delivers to men.

Where are the mystical experiences of our days? In spectator sports, for instance, especially in the intimacy and immediacy with which the TV camera connects us with the action. Exactly, too, with TV soap operas—we are directly connected with the very throb of the otherwise elusive mysteries—just as drama has aspired to from the Greek amphitheater on. Television also connects us with the spellbinding drama of real-life action: a revolution in the making, a tornado as it happens, behind the scene in the workings of political or geological powers. You are *there.* You *are* there. *You* are there.

I think that our work often seems to make the same promise, to offer us a direct personal connection with the powers that govern and sustain life. On the job we abandon ourselves, and find ourselves, in the throbbing stuff of industry, commerce, science, travel, harvest, mining—the primitive powerful energies that make the world spin. Our career promised to give us a front-row seat, a closed-circuit television connection to the main action (a modern equivalent of the old-fashioned pipeline to God). As we came out of adolescence feeling disconnected, partial, not all there, a vocational decision sometimes seemed to offer to change all that. And there were professions and institutions and companies recruiting and seducing with just such promises. On the days when we still get out of bed glad to get up, and go to work with a bounce in our step, that may be what it's about: the feeling that we are about to plunge into something meaningful and powerful and that we will absorb some of the meaning and power. It can sometimes be just that sensual.

I think mystical appetite is part of the reason for our love affair with work—these mystical cravings are powerful and unquenchable—just as I also think believing these promises of mystical connection dooms us to disappointment and grief.

"I do get turned on, sort of, at work, when the mail comes in and I have to start answering it," Len says. "It still takes my breath away a little bit. When I said something like this to my wife once, she got jealous. I suppose any mistress is a quicker turn-on than your wife."

"I think I actually feel homesick away from the job now," Cliff confesses. "It's like being away at camp one summer when I was ten—I feel I really ought to be there and not here." He goes on with another observation of how some parts of the working world seem to offer access to mysteries and powers. "The other night I went to what they call an investment seminar, where some stockbrokers were trying to tell me what to do with my retirement pay. They're a bunch of smooth operators all right, the way they talk about 'pass-through' and 'leverage' and 'liquidity' and all the rest—like a bunch of doctors knowing all the big words for what's wrong with you. It reminded me of the way the Harlem Globetrotters throw the ball around and play tricks with it and have a good time. Or like a magician making coins appear and disappear. These guys really know how money works and they have a good time moving it around. They know they know something special that I don't know, and that turns them on."

"The wood still gives me that good feeling, smelling it, polishing it, shaving it," Andy reports. "But sometimes I admit I can get that same kind of aesthetic experience at my desk. Yeah, opening the mail to see what's coming up is a little like cutting

into wood to find the grain. Making the numbers
balance is like making the table balance. When it's
really going well, my new desk work makes me feel
I'm on a frontier, like a cowboy riding down a
canyon at sunset just feeling good about his job."

Women often get this mystical connection from
other people and from relationships. It seems more
a man's lot to find this connection with the abstrac-
tions and hustle of work life.

And if not *in* the work, then as the *fruit* of work:
Work is the path held out to us for fame or power
or a high standard of living, and that may be enough
to satisfy our mystical cravings for connection and
belonging. Or work may be the prerequisite for the
mystical "oneness" of fulfilling personal relationships. After—and only after—a day of hard work, a
week of hard work, a lifetime of hard work, a man
can claim the relaxation and affection he has earned.
The sad irony is that by then he may have lost touch
with the people who can give it to him.

Work as Monasticism

There is another way men may work "religiously," with intense, narrow, exaggerated commitment.
Work may be religious as a *ritual*. Work may be
religious as a kind of *mysticism*. Work may also be
religious as a form of *monasticism*.

To enter the monastery is to narrow and focus
your life. You choose the dimensions, goals, arenas
of life that seem to have the highest value, the most
transcending, and you dedicate yourself to them.
You withdraw from, seclude yourself from other
rich but, you decide, secondary parts of life. When
you enter a monastery you especially leave behind
emotional involvement with others, personal relationships with family and lovers. You renounce and
peel off those parts of yourself that want to and can
develop those relationships. Working men these

days hardly take the traditional vows of poverty, chastity, and obedience. Indeed, they often understand working as the way to make possible for them a lush and free life exactly the opposite of poverty, chastity, and obedience. But *on the job* there *is* austerity and self-denial. Feelings, personal preferences, values, and loyalties other than those represented by the chosen workplace all tend to give way to the narrowing and focus of work. At a business meeting you can see men parking much of their personality at the door. In a restaurant the men at a business lunch are recognizable by the carefully set ways they are playing their roles.

A monk may seem "spaced out," preoccupied, living in another world, not immediately responsive to ordinary conversation. This is also how people view the working man. The bureaucrat behind the desk seems unresponsive, in a world of his own. Meetings have a strange, inhuman life of their own. And even after hours, when the austerity vows should be lifted, the working man may still seem hard to reach.

If the work keeps going after hours, so does the austerity. Shoptalk controls the dinner party, to the exclusion of the nonworkers present. Shoptalk may even dominate the family conversation, and the narrow, austere, joyless working style may control everything at home, including sex. The working monk avoids intimate personal relationships.

The first monks were loners, hermits, withdrawn in complete austerity from any human contact. (The first syllable of the word "monastic" comes from the Greek word for "single"—as in "monotheism," for example.) Then monks banded together, but as a way of reinforcing their aloneness rather than modifying it. So when men band together at work, they are more often trading reminders of their emotional austerity than breaking it down; they are joining a band of loners.

If work is a monastic refuge for men who choose
seclusion from women and the emotional entangle-
ments that seem to go with them, that must be a big
reason why there seem to be walls around this monastery called work and signs that say *No Women
Admitted*. The discrimination women experience as
a denial of power, as exclusion from an elite, is just
that of course. It also may be a way to protect an
emotionally austere monastic retreat that men have
come to rely on. To enter successfully, women often
have to adopt the same emotional austerity, like
sneaking admittance to a medieval monastery by
wearing straight-cut men's clothing.

Why do monks, whether medieval or modern—
whether they are accountants, authors, or auto
mechanics, cowboys, drill press operators, or engineers—*why* do they choose narrowing and focusing,
seclusion and emotional austerity? Is the renunciation for the sake of the commitment to work, as the
monks are likely to say? Do we have to give up emotional life in order to get the job done? Or could it
also be the other way around: the focus on work
permits retreat from emotional life? I think the monasticism of work may be so important to men because
there is important emotional release in emotional
withdrawal. A man goes out his front door Monday
morning for many reasons and feeling many things,
and it is certainly too strong to say that many men
are fleeing, but the monastic life that lies ahead at
work may feel very welcome to him after the weekend encounters. That welcome is an important satisfaction, binding him to his work.

The monastic "vows" may have been made back
in junior high school or even earlier, when work—
whether schoolwork in the classroom, homework,
a workout in the gym, or an after-school job—
afforded welcome relief from the relentlessly awk-
ward humiliation of trying to come to terms with
the girls in his life and the feelings they provoked.

That relief could keep somebody stubbornly at work for a long time.

People like Len and Cliff don't have much to say on this topic. The way things are with the people at home is about the last thing men talk about when they get together. That's understandable, if getting together has the point of leaving the people at home behind.

It's like any other phobia: If I make a point of walking around ladders, not under them, and I avoid bad luck, I'm likely to continue making the trip around the ladder. If I fear falling from high places, that fear is comfortably dealt with if I avoid high places, so I stubbornly stay on the ground. If my work helps me deal with whatever pain or difficulty I find in loving, parenting, or meeting any other emotional demand—largely by avoiding it—I'm going to cling pretty closely to my work. Beyond this, if work does fix some things in my life by giving me a place to retreat to, I may come to expect work to fix everything in my life, so work becomes a permanent way of life, a sure fixer, a general therapy, a religion.

3
Trying to Work Past Grief

It is time, halfway through this book, to remember that it is called *"when* work goes sour." Perhaps it could also be called *"How* work goes sour," or maybe *"If."* But the book is not called "Work *does* go sour." Probably most men are happy with their work much of the time, and some men all of the time, and I have no desire to persuade them otherwise, only to celebrate the contentment and "rightness" of work when it is there—when a man's work fits him, suits him, moves him with his dreams, not against them.

But when work does pain and thwart, when it makes a man feel like a misfit, out of step with himself, then it is time to pay attention. If we notice what is happening (chapter 1), try to understand how it comes to happen (chapter 2), it is then time to notice how we respond—not always too well. This third chapter will look at some of our most common reactions when work goes sour, many of them defensive and not very helpful.

"When the going gets tough, the tough get going." That's the usual male strategy, men redoubling their efforts against challenge. It is the strategy on which men break themselves.

Men may be alone among the creatures of the world in attempting this strategy. It is not very prev-

alent, because it does not prevail. The strategy that
succeeds is: "When the going gets tough, the tough
let themselves be vulnerable, and they change." He
who would save his life must lose it. There is more
about this in the next chapter, where we talk about
"conversion" and "liberation." Mentioning it here,
however, helps us to understand, by stark contrast,
the array of stubborn ways men deal with grief by
redoubling the very efforts that gave them grief.
When work goes sour, many men *work* all the
harder.

We live in the midst of a world in which maladjustment is not rare, avoidable, or even unwelcome.
Indeed, among the species with which we share
Creation and in the legends of our own species, the
experience of being a misfit, out of place and out of
step with one's surroundings, is precisely what fuels
and directs growth, discovery, evolution. For plants
and animals it is called adapting and evolving. For
humans it is called invention, exploration, heroism.
It might just as well be called "conversion." When
old ways, old patterns, the old self prove disrupting
and distressing, they are given up and new patterns
and new selfhood are discovered. When seeds are
blown to alien soil or animals are forced to migrate,
when the climate changes, when food supplies disappear and new predators appear, plants and animals that persist in their old patterns—stubbornly
"protecting their identity"—disappear. Those that
survive and thrive are those that abandon the very
foraging habits or foliage patterns that had defined
them, made them what they were. They give up deep
roots, wide leaves, daytime feeding, or whatever
and find new life-styles. They adapt. They convert.
He who would save his life must lose it.

Christians believe that God works with special
energy and caring to create and redeem precisely
in settings of maladjustment and forsakenness. They
believe this from looking at the abundant creative

energy with which the ecology tries to restore itself: lakes have good ability to clean themselves; species adapt with marvelous inventiveness. Christians believe this from looking at prevailing biblical images of the settings in which God most evidently functions, in wilderness, exile, crucifixion, among the dispossessed and outcast. Christians believe this from examining their own experiences of conversion, the renewing grace that surprises and sustains just when one feels misplaced or misunderstood and acknowledges it. In the traditional pattern of the conversion experience, one yields one's own efforts to define and defend and establish oneself. In "surrendering," one is "surprised by grace." New avenues, new patterns of life that had been blocked from view by the old patterns and by efforts to preserve them now present themselves.

This is probably the conversion that men need when work goes sour. Men need to surrender the commitments and habits of work—even though these have been the prime defining characteristics of their manhood—*especially* because these have been their prime defining characteristics. Drive, analyze, control, master. When the center of life goes sour, it must be time to change the center of life.

But the problem is, obviously, that the only thing more painful than having the center of life go sour is having to surrender that center. From a distance, we can admire and celebrate the plants, animals, or other heroes who have "converted," have surrendered identities gone sour and discovered new lives. But up close, in the midst of sourness, facing the need for conversion and surrender, the yielding of the very commitments and efforts into which we have most heavily invested our very being, is excruciatingly painful. It's like having one's skin peeled off, raw. This is precisely the kind of vulnerability— the vulnerability that men, especially working men, most need—that men, especially working men, find so intolerable. The same relentless, habitual rut that has turned things sour (when they go sour) is turned to, clung to—just when surrender is most needed—for cure and remedy. Species that do this don't seem to survive.

The final two chapters will try to hold out some possibilities for such vulnerability and conversion. When Atlas gets cramps from holding up the world, *maybe* he can let go and make two remarkable discoveries: that the world remains intact without him and—even more remarkable—that he has alternative ways to live his life. This chapter will survey, with a blend of impatience and compassion, some of the ways in which we men turn to more work to remedy the distress of discovering that work goes sour, what Atlas does before he lets go.

Redoubling Our Effort

It is like reaching for a drink to cure the hangover left by too much drink. It is like prescribing more medication to undo the side effects produced by overmedication. It is like issuing new memoranda or regulations or writing new legislation to try to correct ambiguities and close loopholes created by past memoranda or regulations or legislation. It is like escalating a war in Vietnam or Nicaragua to correct the dilemmas and undo the pain left by the war so far.

It is like the man, beginning to find flaws in the new car of his choice or reading appealing advertisements for other cars, who redoubles his loyalty, discovering still more virtues in the car of his choice and scoffing at the challenges.

It is like responding to the incineration of *Challenger* and its crew with the same engineering and management talents that caused it, all for the purpose of launching the next flight as soon as possible.

It is like the man at the wheel who sets out to find a street in a strange part of town. "It should be right about here," he says, holding his course. If it isn't, he says it again, circling the same block, or darts off on a new hunch that is a close version of the first one. When his own scheme is failing, he is least open to any suggestions from his passengers, especially the suggestion that he stop and ask directions. Such vulnerability, such conversion, is what a man may tolerate least just when he most needs it—probably *because* he most needs it. Need is intolerable.

When work goes sour and leaves us pained and needy, especially in need of newness and change, that is when we firm up the postures of work. Just when we need to surrender, to be open to surprise, we reenact the old rhythms of work, which are the opposite of surrender. When the work goes sour, we see *this* as a new *task* to deal with. There is some new puzzle to solve, and we must do it and do it right. We must prove that we are bigger than the problem. We must be able to wrap it up, put it in a box, make it surrender to us. We must master it. We must work at it, or else we are lost. For working has become, literally, our way of life.

The "conversion" we need when work goes sour depends on accepting the fact that the work has indeed gone sour (just as any effective grief work depends on accepting the fact of the loss). Most of the strategies we actually follow, which this chapter will describe, are intended to cover up the fact of sourness, the failure (just as so many ineffective attempts at dealing with grief deny the loss). It is very hard to admit the failure of work. We have so identified our self with our work, become so dependent on our work for a guarantee of selfhood, that if our work fails—if this emperor has no clothes—we feel naked. Without work, we feel we are nobody.

It is easier to think of *myself* as a failure—and, as we shall see, this is exactly one of our moves when work goes sour—than to admit that work has failed me. The liberation we need, as we shall discuss later, lies in exactly the opposite move—in discovering that I am somebody even without my work, that I need not bind my fate to the fate of my work, or my well-being to my work's capacity to nurture and assure me. I need to be able to let go of work and working not so much because it is a futile means of salvation as because it is unnecessary. The well-being of my life is already assured, if I will only recognize it.

But compared with such open, trusting liberation, here are some of the strategies we actually employ.

Blaming Others

If something goes wrong, if our work proves dissatisfyingly sour, we can explain *why*. We can write a script that makes our distress seem understandable and logical, account for how it got that way and what can be done next. The script takes work and agility, but most of us are good at it. We construct a world which makes our distress an orderly part of an orderly history. Most often that history blames others, but contriving the orderly history may be more important than placing blame.

When Len feels thwarted by discovering his reports often go unheeded, he *knows* what has happened and the knowing puts him in charge again. "They don't know what they're doing" is a simple and satisfying script, sometimes embellished with "They can't keep track of what they've assigned me" or even "They don't really know enough to understand what somebody's saying who does understand things." The last script gives his own experience a clearer and more focused role.

If you encounter someone labeled by a psychiatrist as a paranoid schizophrenic, you are meeting someone who is working hard and well with energy and talent and effect. Not unlike an accountant or auto mechanic or engineer or physician or most any other worker, the paranoiac is dealing with problems by rearranging his world—devising a history—in a way that identifies a cause and a solution, some well-defined objective or challenge to be attacked or fended off. Every worker is a kind of Rambo, identifying an enemy to be challenged or thwarted. The paranoid worker is successfully coping with disappointment or failure or fear or threat by wrapping it in an intricately woven web, reconstructing reality in such a way that the problems are all sufficiently objective, external, easy to identify and easy to deal with. That's not much different from what most of us do when we are most disappointed and pained. Our paranoia is mild enough to be regarded as normal and standard—which it is. Blaming outward is a very effective defense against facing the truth that something very close to us has gone sour.

"I guess Ronnie is just troubled and upset today, maybe by something his mother said," Paul concludes after his own efforts to work at parenting fail abysmally. "This business just generates too much inefficient paperwork. Everybody wants memos and reports without knowing what they're doing." That is Len's understanding of the trap he is in, carefully avoiding any thought that might point to his own addiction to pushing paper.

Work and working are honored as the measure of all things, never challenged, never relativized. "Work" is judge, never the judged. We may turn on other tyrannical judges—father, boss—and judge them, but seldom the tyrant of work itself. The others who are blamed, the bosses, the system, the son, are judged for failing to fit effectively into the scheme of work. If Ronnie is restless with the "working" way of building and flying a kite, so that the whole experience becomes unsatisfactory for Paul, Paul doesn't consider Ronnie's restlessness as a warning about work (along with his own dissatisfaction). Ronnie's restlessness, no more than his own dissatisfaction, is not allowed to judge working. Instead, working remains the criterion, and Ronnie's restlessness is judged by that. If Ronnie doesn't fit into working, *he* must have a problem.

In the same way, one's own dissatisfaction never becomes the signal to bring relativizing and remedial judgment to bear on working. Instead, if I am dissatisfied, then maybe I have a problem. This takes us to our next category.

Blaming Self

When work goes sour, men are quick to blame others for the pain and the maladjustment they feel. Men are also quick to blame themselves, at least secretly. It can be quite devastating and depressing self-blame: "I guess I'm just getting old. . . . I don't seem to be up to it. . . . I don't know how to get a kick out of life anymore. . . . I don't really deserve any better. . . . I'm lucky they didn't find out sooner what an imposter I am."

It might seem that blaming the self is the opposite of blaming others and that the same man could hardly do both. But in fact men do send blame outward and inward, play both victim and villain, often at the same time. Paul, who is ready to blame Ronnie and his mother for the kite-flying failure, also harbors some self-devastating thoughts which he will share with us when he knows us better, such as "I'm probably not a very good father. . . . Maybe I just shouldn't have kids." Blaming yourself is not so very different from blaming others, really. It is another way of *working* on the problem, arranging the world in an orderly way so that there is an easy target—which just happens to be yourself.

Blaming yourself, just like blaming others, mostly serves the purpose of deflecting blame from the real culprit, work itself. The last thing Paul is able to say to himself is to acknowledge that the "working" style with which he goes about parenting is the problem. That would require a change, a conversion, of something he feels to be a precious, necessary, and inevitable part of himself. Working is not something he does; work is something he is. It is far easier to feel inadequate as a parent or as a worker than to feel not a worker at all.

Someone who is retired, like Cliff, especially knows how that is: Deny the abrupt change from being worker to nonworker. Tell everyone you are busier than ever. Continue working, compulsively, at every chore you can find, including removing every piece of ice from the neighbor's walk. Blame your arthritis or your age or the weather or your wife because you feel down and without energy or joy; don't blame the work or lack of it or the failure of a lifetime career to deliver satisfaction.

When women are battered by men it seems unaccountable—and terribly sad—that so many so often defend and protect the batterer. They fail to report the incident. They explain away the bruises as a "fall." They blame themselves—quite unjustifiably—for provoking the assault. They excuse the assault—"He was drunk." Just like men battered by work, they are often more ready to blame themselves than to blame the actual culprit. For the same revealingly sad reasons, when women deflect blame from the batterer and spread it in all other directions, it is because they are so dependent on the batterer. Perhaps it is a psychological dependence, perhaps an economic dependence—they have no other options than to remain dependent on the man's financial support—or most likely a combination of psychological and economic dependence. They need to protect the object of that dependence.

I think that men protect their work and their postures of working in just the same way and for just the same reasons. Instead of placing responsibilities for their pain on work and working, they deflect blame in all other directions. For men are at least as dependent, psychologically and economically, on work as some women are on their husbands. Work has become a psychological addiction; it has become—or so we think—the only option. We feel sentenced—a lifetime sentence—to our work, just as the battered woman feels sentenced—a lifetime sentence—to living with the husband. A woman often requires a long and painful transition before she can experience the conversion of understanding herself as someone able to live her own life without the habitual man. It may take years of dreadful battering, long isolated shelter, and weaning with massive support, psychologically and financially. It probably is even a longer and more difficult process for a man to convert, to be weaned from the battering of workplace and work and working postures.

The man ready to spread blame outward or turn it on himself, even at great discomfort, in order to protect the real culprit—work—on which he is so dependent and with which he is so totally identified, is just like the alcoholic. The alcoholic works hard to identify all the causes of his loss of friends, his failing health, and his other distress. He may even attack himself—"I don't deserve friends"—before he will face the fact that his reliance on alcohol is causing the problem. Same with our dependence on work, no matter how much it actually fails us.

Homework

When work goes sour, men take their work home. Sometimes literally, a full briefcase or a floppy disk, demanding time and quiet—sometimes a modem—

competing with family and relaxation, as though more of the wrestling with this angel (work) will make it yield the blessing denied during the day. But more often the homework is not more of the wrestling with papers and telephone and keyboard that defeated the day. Instead, men take home "working" as a style of life, as a posture, as a habit, as a script for home or family, as a way to do ham radio or gardening, church or lodge, Scouts or Little League, parenting kids or making love, jogging or even fishing. None of these new arenas *has* to be a workplace. In fact, they are all better approached without the posture and rhythms of work. But they all do, very frequently, become workplaces—goals set, tasks assigned to self and others, strategy to be developed, and fervent commitment to successful accomplishment. Even the fish lure must be cast "right," and your son must score and triumph in the Little League game. You must set up these targets and then strain until you hit them. Work, floundering in the daily workplace, is moved to smaller, more confined places, where it may not belong but where it can thrive more surely. Home becomes a sheltered workshop for the refugee worker.

As work has grown more complex technically and has become more entangled in alienating social structures, and therefore has become more sour more often, men have resorted increasingly to specialization as a kind of refuge. They carve out a small piece of work, more confined, more manageable, more promising of some satisfaction. They find a target easier to hit, a checklist more readily checked off—since work is a matter of scoring and scorekeeping. So in their workplace, men narrow their assignment, limit their aspiration, confine the challenge. So lawyers and physicians take certain kinds of cases and not others. Appliance repairmen and automobile mechanics work on some models and not others, or on transmissions but not carburetors. Men who wait on restaurant tables serve food *or* wine *or* clear the dishes. (A waitress is more likely to do it all.)

When a man makes a work project out of a deacons' pancake breakfast at church or coaching his son in Little League baseball or filing his income tax, I think it is much the same kind of specialization. It is focusing on a target much easier to hit and focusing energies, including all those energies frustrated in the workplace, on hitting it. "We've *got* to get the pancake reservations in a week in advance, and the cooks *must* be there by six thirty in the morning." "Keep your eyes glued to that ball and get your bat off your shoulder." "I have to have the den for the entire weekend so I can lay out all the receipts and bank statements and get this tax return knocked off." These focus on the narrow targets, demanding and trying to guarantee satisfaction, unleashing the intensity and urgency built up out of other work frustrations. Things have to go right. Others must play successful parts in this urgent script. This imposition of intense work postures and expectations on situations that are not inherently work situations and on people who have not agreed to be working partners—this deserves the word "macho," the pushing around of others to fit one's own needs.

Boss, Helper, Expert, Judge

Another kind of specialization or displacement for targeting is still more common, more subtle, more damaging to all concerned, and therefore more important to talk about here. This is the specialization of working posture, a distinct role men choose to take in relationship to others. Whether it is at home or at church, on a golf course or on the Little League field, whether with family or with friends or even with strangers, a man may choose to play out the role of Boss or Helper or Expert or Judge. These are all specialized working postures. They give a well-defined fixed target, a limited checklist. A man becomes adept at performing one of these specialized roles and persists in it.

Homework: Boss

Some men choose to be boss, or maybe general. In whatever situation, they will command or instruct others in how to behave. The work is in arranging the behavior of the others, and the success and satisfaction is found in their compliance—or apparent compliance. (People who live with bosses learn that distinction between compliance and apparent compliance much more readily than the bosses do.) The boss instructs his wife and children what to wear and when to cut their hair. He insists that the church committee meeting follow a rigid agenda, and he fumes when conversation strays or becomes inefficient—he wants the job done. He coaches, very explicitly, the politicians and the football players on his TV, and may explode when they don't comply.

"When we have company in for dinner, I get impatient when my wife doesn't get it served on time," Len confesses. "I get out there in the kitchen and I start saying, 'Why didn't you put that water on to boil sooner?' and 'Let's lay all six plates out here on the counter and then we can serve everything at once and get it out onto the table.'"

Somebody tells Len, "That sounds pretty macho. How do you get away with it?" But someone else says, "It sounds like you feel on the spot, very responsible, as though the guests will blame *you* if the supper is not on time. That's a big load to carry." "Yeah," Len replies softly. "A bigger load than I *can* carry. I guess I feel like that a lot." The fragility and vulnerability underneath the bossing is not hard to find. It is an anxiety induced as a casualty of working. Len feels "at work," responsible, all the time. He's all the more anxious about making the dinner party work well because he's feeling bruised from the daytime work going sour. "It's up to me, but maybe I'm not up to it, so I must try all the harder." That's the way it feels, and "trying all the harder" takes the form of bossing. It's just because he feels pushed around that he must push back and push others around. It's just because he feels downed that he must get himself up, even at the cost of putting down his wife. It's because he feels weak that he comes on strong. The man wounded by being bossed—worked over—bosses others. Though relying on work is exactly what has left Len stranded, feeling unsure and unsafe, it is all he knows to try to make himself feel more sure and more safe. So he works. He bosses.

Homework: Helper

Though bossing is an obvious way of bringing work home, of making work work better at home than it does at work, why speak of helping in the same way? Because helping, as usually practiced by men, is another form of bossing, another form of working, another form of making oneself feel in charge, safe, sure, responsible, effective, successful, even at the expense of someone else, of keeping someone else down, worked over, worked against. Men make work out of their helping. It becomes relentless, insistent, targeted. "I must shovel all the snow off the walk, and I need the Johnsons to know it." That's the straightforward way Cliff goes about his helping, and so do most of the rest of us. We rely on the helping, on having it acknowledged and successful. The other must be helped and must know it. Len's maneuvers in the kitchen could be thought of as helping fully as much as bossing. Indeed, that is how he thought of them.

Helping, like any other form of work, especially work brought home, is following a script: There is someone who has a problem and needs help, so the helper rides onstage with the power and goodness of heart and the perfect timing to solve the problem and bring about a happy ending. All work is, in a sense, a variation on this script: There is a cast of characters, there is a problem, and there is something very clearly to be done about it, with results that can be seen and appreciated. So one reason the helper helps is that this is a well-defined and familiar script, and a worker likes scripts.

More than this, the helping script lets the helper be the star. That role is welcome when such experience is in short supply.

But still more important, especially for the man who may feel ejected from all scripts, is that the helper is guaranteed a place in the cast. If I am unsure of a place in any meaningful script, a place in people's lives, I can guarantee that place by creating a need and moving to fill it. There is always snow to be shoveled from *somebody's* walk, some delinquency or difficulty of a wife or child to be corrected, some errand to be run, some chore to be done, some good deed to be performed. For the one who feels sidelined, helping may be the easiest and surest way to get into the action. For each helper who feels thwarted and defeated, another person can always be found who is in need of a good deed, a good deed the helper can turn into a successful feat. Joseph built a career dutifully running helpful errands and offering helpful advice, pleasing one father figure after another—or trying to.

What if the people at home don't feel in need, don't want to be part of that script, are not asking for a helper? They must be recruited to play their part in the script. They must be taught to be in need, to be helpees. The helper is good at this recruiting, at defining and diagnosing and even inducing neediness in those at home, a neediness to give him, as helper, something to work on. "It's true, I never asked the Johnsons if they wanted their walk cleaned, let alone so thoroughly. That was just in my head," Cliff reflects. And Len brings himself to admit that everyone else seemed to be relaxed about supper and not anxious about getting it served and eaten on time. "In fact, maybe my own anxiety got my wife upset and rattled—to give me something to rescue her from." (Did someone say, "Sounds like blaming the victim"?) The helper needs a helpee, a target for his work of helping, and part of the work is in "helping" those at home to discover their need. Much that is often called chauvinism, from holding chairs and doors to more significant put-downs, comes about because men, on the rebound from work turned sour, need a script and a starring role, and one of the most familiar and accustomed scripts is that of helper and helpee.

What an irony—indeed, how tragic—that this scramble for place by the work of helping impedes the finding of a genuine place in the life at home. Neither the man nor those at home can find the connections of partnership and mutuality and intimacy and vulnerability (the opening of genuine needs to each other, not manufactured needs), so long as the man relies on working scripts. The helper manufactures a sense of self and a sense of place, a sense of home, but they never satisfy. That requires the man being himself, helpless when he is, helping only as requested.

Homework: Expert

Len recalls an incident recently when his wife had a bad headache. He told her she had been worrying too much about their teenage son and to pour herself a good drink and try to relax. "I didn't tell her I was sorry that her head was hurting," Len recalls in telling this incident. "I didn't even offer to pour the drink myself or to rub her neck—not even to be a 'helper.' " He *explained* her headache to her and how to remedy it. He *worked* on her headache—as an expert.

"My daughter came in the den and stopped still to listen to the music that was playing," Andy is reminded. When his daughter said, "That's beautiful!" what was Andy's response? Not "I like it too" or "Does it make pictures in your head?" or "Do you want to move the needle back to the start so we can hear the whole thing together?" It was "That's Mendelssohn's piano trio." It's so much easier to be at work—as an expert, in this case—than to share the delight.

"Ronnie got excited about hearing a birdcall in the back yard the other day," Paul remembers. "He tried to whistle like the bird. What I did was name the bird for him and explain why it was singing. 'It's a cardinal, and it sits up on top of that tree to tell all the other birds that that is its tree.' "

Same when Andy's daughter came to him tearful and sober about some street crime she had seen on TV—whether it was news or "drama," Andy wasn't sure. "I didn't try to hear her pain or even try to comfort her. I just explained that is how some people behave, in some parts of the city, but it probably wouldn't happen to her."

Maybe the most dramatic moment in Joseph's story is the reunion with his father after years of separation when his father thought him dead. When the father arrived in Egypt, he threw his arms around Joseph and wept and said, " 'I am ready to die, now that I have seen you and know that you are still alive.' Then Joseph said to his brothers and the rest of his father's family, 'I will go and tell the king' " (Gen. 46:30–31). That's his only recorded greeting: my son the bureaucrat.

"If I had been more relaxed about how things

were going at work, I might have been more able to be open to my daughter," Andy reflects. Which maybe is another way of saying that work going sour gets brought home.

Becoming an expert—knowing, explaining, diagnosing, prescribing, labeling, having an answer for everything—what an easy and natural way to make work out of anything, and a common way; probably all men do it. Stay responsible, keep every situation scripted, targeted, under control, worked on. As the scientist on the job risks missing the wonder of it all, and the lawyer risks missing the pathos, any man can make a science or a law of anything. If your wife confronts you in anger, you can become expert *about* her anger. No need to deal with it as anger when you can deal with it as specimen, a case, something to be worked on, to be explained. "It must be that time of the month" or "Women are so emotional" are two of the most notorious "expert" explanations. Slightly more refined may be such "expert" wisdom as "The kid must really have got you down today" or "Have you noticed that this is one kind of issue you really have trouble handling?" The expert is careful never to respond to situations with wonder or surprise or feelings, never with appreciation for the poetry of experience, but with analysis and literalness and linear rationality. Life has its own script, its own inevitability—"working"—and its script can be known, can be absorbed into your own script. You can be an expert. Especially with the daily events of home and family you can be an expert. That is most appealing when there are questions about your expertise, and much else, on the job.

As with bossing and helping and other forms of work brought home, being expert can provide a one-two boost, a one-two punch. There is reassurance to the self from the sense of working, doing a job, checking something off, hitting a target, obeying a script. There can also be the extra boost that comes from putting another down. Like bossing and helping, experting can be a put-down. It need not be but it can be. The expert can be signaling that what he knows is something you should know but don't. "That singing bird is a cardinal, dummy" can be the full message, even without the last word. It can be said impatiently. It can be said matter-of-factly, in a tone that says "everyone knows this, of course." It can be said heavily and firmly in a way that belittles the other's delight or wonder or curiosity or despair or anger, or whatever the feelings are that are being Saran-wrapped by the expert's pronouncement. At home as on the job, working can be highly competitive.

Homework: Judge

The expert works with facts and objectivity. The judge works with opinions, is more explicitly competitive, and is much more intentionally belittling, putting down. Otherwise, the work of the judge is much like the work of the expert. Life has a script, not of facts this time but of good and bad, right and wrong, and the work consists of knowing and announcing this script at every opportunity. No openness to uncertainty and ambiguity, to debate or to change, the work of judging is to eliminate such openness. The judge's checklist of work is to remove ambiguities, to settle doubts, to correct error, to right wrong, to answer questions, to convert heresy, to enlist converts, to make rules and obey them.

It may be the essence of work to squeeze and chop life into pieces small enough to fit agendas and checklists, formulas and recipes, tables of organizations, measurable criteria for success—to collapse experiences into something that can be counted, controlled, solved, constricted. A man at home faces a wealth of new experience: expanding horizons, through the lives of his wife and children, his church and neighborhood, even the newspaper and television he encounters at home. The judge declines these invitations to new experience. He *works* on these possibilities by leashing them to systems and frameworks already familiar and established. New music, new ideas, new folk heroes brought into the house by children or media or spouse—these are not to be opened to, listened to, learned from. That would be play, not work. That would require surrender of a kind recommended in the next chapter. That would assume trust. Instead, these new experiences are to be arrayed on an established framework. Where they don't fit, they are pronounced misfits. The judge is passing along the treatment he receives at work. "You're not driving the best route to get downtown. . . . The new mayor is crazy. . . . I really wish you wouldn't spend so much time with that set of friends. . . . How can you spend money going to listen to that music all night? . . . I think you ought to be thinking about a more realistic career. . . . Shouldn't you be spending less time on the telephone and less time at the television? . . . Divestment is just not a realistic idea. . . . " This is the way the judge works on those at home.

The judge is quick to evaluate, and quick to condemn novelty and change as negative. To be open to novelty, to leave any questions of judgment open, is not to have anything to work on, not to get work done.

All of us have our moods of wanting to be boss or trying to be helper or needing to parade our expertise or to pronounce judgment. Probably men more than women, because men may be more likely to need to perform and accomplish measurable tasks and to guarantee a place in some known script. But it is especially when men are bruised on the job, or made to feel abandoned, or made unsure of them-

selves in one of the many other ways that work
delivers its jolts—these are the times that men especially fall back on these familiar routines and take
their work home, much to their own damage and to
the forfeit of the nurture and support they could find
at home: if they would be open to it.

This discussion of "homework" is, in part, adapted from the chapter
"Crippled Cripplers" in my *The Male Predicament* (San Francisco:
Harper & Row, 1985). In that chapter especially "helping" and "know-
ing" are seen as subtle macho techniques.

4

Conversion and Liberation

Give two schoolboys the two ends of a rope with a knot in the middle. Draw a line on the ground in front of each boy. Tell the boys, "You get a nickel every time you can pull the knot across your line." For you and for me and for most boys we know and were, this becomes competitive tug-of-war. We assume a scarcity of nickels. We assume that for me to get my nickel I must keep you from getting yours. So we strain and compete. We work. I may drag the knot across my line a few times, working against your best efforts, and vice versa. In ten minutes maybe one boy wins five nickels and feels triumphant, and the other boy wins four nickels and feels defeated. That's the way work is.

Give the same rope, draw the same lines, offer the same nickels to two other boys, perhaps Latin Americans on the streets of Spanish Harlem in New York or somewhere in Central America. They don't "work." They play. Probably with music in their voice and dance in their step, they saw the rope back and forth across their two lines at a great pace and in steady rhythm. In ten minutes they can make twenty-five dollars each. They are not tricking you or outsmarting you—although these encounters between differing cultures can easily make both sides feel suspicious or duped. They are following your

rules honestly in the way that makes the most sense
to them. They just naturally envision the situation
differently. They assume plenty of nickels, they
assume a "user friendly" assignment, and they assume collaboration and partnership. It never occurs
to them to make the assumptions that you and I
make automatically—the assumption of competition, the assumption that we must wrestle an unwill-
ing and unfriendly piece of work to yield something
of personal value, my assumption that you are out
to stop me and that I must therefore stop you first,
the mentality of preemptive strike, the shoot-out at
high noon, which is the essence of machismo, the
swagger and the bluff of the man who feels that
everything is at stake and he does not have what it
takes. It doesn't occur to them to "work" with the
rope.

The first two boys, you and I, work with the rope.
The second two get the job done far better without
"working" at all. The first two assume that the job is
bigger and tougher than they are—as most of us
assume about our jobs—and that they must struggle
against odds, prove themselves, throw all of themselves against the job and maybe still be found wanting. The second two think they are bigger than the
job, so they can relax and even be playful. I think
the main difference between the two pairs of boys is
in how they feel about themselves, whether they
think of themselves as small or big, as alone and
tested against huge odds, or as partnered and buoyed
and competent. I think that our liberation from the
grief of work, yours and mine, lies in discovering
the secret of the second pair of boys: Work can be
done—better—when done more playfully, and it
can be done more playfully when we feel better
about ourselves. That's the simple secret, but it
requires a huge conversion in the way we feel about
ourselves.

Some of you may read this far and object. "I don't

want my surgeon or airline pilot to be playful at his work." But I think you do, we all do. Not irresponsible and reckless, of course. But not wrestling, in a tug-of-war contest with our appendix or our airplane. It is precisely the relaxed, unfrenzied—yes, playful—manner of our surgeon (like Alan Alda's character in M*A*S*H) or of the pilot on the loudspeaker that communicates just the sense of competence and self-assurance with which the playful boys with the rope earned their fifty dollars. When I am allowed to listen in to the pilot-to-controller conversations approaching LaGuardia airport and the pilot is told to turn left at the Statue of Liberty and follow a heading of 10 degrees, I feel better if my pilot responds whimsically, "Left at the Lady, and up the river" than if he responds woodenly. But, more to the point in this chapter, so does he, I think. It reminds him, as it reminds me, that he feels bigger than his work.

Liberation lies in a change of *attitude* about work, resulting from a change of attitude about *self*. Liberation does not lie in quitting work; when work goes sour, some men dream of being rid of it, escaping the pain of work by not working. They look forward to leaving the job at the end of the day, or for vacation, or for retirement; or they want to move from one job to another; or they plan to leave the chores of house and yard and move into a condominium. Such changes of scene, such rhythms of rest alternating with work, are essential. But they don't really deal with the problem.

For one thing, as Paul has made clear, working men too readily work at their rest and play. But, more important, the work goes on; we men will continue to spend a major part of our lives at work; we need to and want to. The question is, How can we work with less pain, less addiction, less eroding intensity? How can we become the equivalent, in our working, of the social drinker, one who can take it or leave it? If work is oppressive, the answer must be not so much to eliminate the work as to eliminate the oppressiveness.

What we need more than a change of scene or a change of task is a change of attitude, a change of style, a change of the *way* we go about things, a change in the way we think about ourselves as we approach an activity or rest time. We need relief not so much from the drudgery of our work as from the power over our lives and well-being we have given to working as a style of life; freedom from the devotion we give to work. We need replacement for the picture of ourselves as nothing but worker.

Men will continue to have jobs to do: pushing paper and snow shovels and lawn mowers, pushing ideas against resistant bosses and institutions, pushing the myriad other wheels and levers that make up workday responsibilities and home-time chores. Men will continue to wage and lose political battles, to hope for far more from their place of work than it can deliver, to give more than they get. Men will continue to feel unappreciated and disappointed. But is there a mood of liberation in which these things happen as a matter of course without being devastating? Can the work routinely unroll its script, including the inevitable disappointments, without feeling sour?

Is there a liberated way of doing tasks which lets a man approach and leave the tasks with lightness, not with heaviness; with sweetness, not sourness; as though the tasks are smaller than he is, not larger; as tasks he chooses rather than tasks he is chained to? Whereas men now too often work at their play, is there some way men can come to play at their work, to work with a sense that the work is not the end-all and be-all of life? Could pieces of work, whether writing a report or designing a machine or repairing a faucet, be something more like watching a football game or playing a game of Ping-Pong, something you do for a time with a bit of relish; then leave behind, don't lose sleep over. Maybe we first need to liberate the TV football and the Ping-Pong game from a relentless sense of working.

When women talk about liberating themselves from reliance on men's expectations, they sometimes mean separating themselves from men, as some men might want to separate themselves from work. But more often they mean just changing their attitudes ("just?") about their relations with men. They mean to withdraw some of the power over their lives they have given men. They mean to become less dependent, less reliant on offering devoted service in exchange for presumed promises of goodwill. When women talk about liberation, they talk about changing their attitudes about themselves as they go about their daily life, not so much changing the personnel and activity of that daily life. A woman might make the liberating discovery, for example, that it is *not* crucial to her sense of well-being after all to have the house immaculate and gourmet food waiting for her husband's five-thirty homecoming and to have his approval for this. Even after such "liberation" she still may choose to clean and cook, but without the desperation and urgency, without "working" at it. Her well-being has other sources. That's what I think men might mean about thinking about liberation from working. I don't *need* working, I just do it.

Portrait of the Liberated Man

The dictionary says that work is mental or physical labor in order to achieve something. To find liberation from work is not to change the first part, the exertion or effort. We just find occasional moments of rest or play to give us relief. But I think liberation from work softens the meaning of the last part of the definition, "in order to achieve something." It is the intensity of directing, of aiming at a target, the intensity of needing to produce or accomplish something—that is what sets up work to go sour. Can we work, can we live without needing so much to control and guarantee the outcome, without needing to direct or to produce or to accomplish, without needing to be "right," without needing to be "best"? Can we stop measuring ourselves against standards of direction and production that always defeat us? Can we yield the responsibility and let ourselves participate instead? Can we enjoy the process more than needing the product?

Unliberated, we easily think of ourselves as like the giant wheel of a mill, the wheel that supplies all the energy to keep the machinery inside functioning. That's an awesome responsibility. Putting out the energy necessary to keep the machinery going can never be adequately done or appreciated. Liberated, can we think of ourselves, on the job or at home, as being steadily and gently moved by a reliable flow of water filling the fins of the wheel, one after the other, and keeping us—and the machinery—going?

The facts of work won't change, but their effect on us may change because our attitudes toward them change when our attitude toward ourself changes. We are not small and delinquent. The good things of this life—the love of others, the sense of self-worth, of integrity and identity and direction, the feelings of harmony and engagement with the world around us, and with God—these things are not scarce, not to be competed for. They are plentiful and assured. We need not compete, just as we cannot achieve these good things by our own exertion, our own work, our own contrivances and strategy. Indeed, these exertions separate us from the good things, by measuring and perpetuating the distance between ourselves and them.

We don't need to best others to win these good

things. Indeed, others are our companions, not adversaries; in solidarity with them, the good things are more plentiful and available than in competition with them.

Our exertion, our work, is not *prior* to a sense of well-being, not a *means* to it. Some would say the work is an expression of the sense of well-being; it follows *from* it. I think it is more true to say that, in liberation, our work is *irrelevant* to the sense of well-being, to the sense of salvation and harmony within ourselves and with the world around us and with God. We can think about this well-being and harmony without having to think about our work. We can experience well-being regardless of what we experience in our work. We don't *need* our work for anything fundamentally important. We are already established as persons of worth and stature. We can hold up our head as we go to work, not cringe and hope that the work will go so well that we can hold up our head afterward.

First, I think, our attitude toward ourself changes, then our attitude toward work. If I feel befriended—assuredly befriended by whatever is important to me, God, family, or friends, the community and all those who somehow seem to be looking over my shoulder—then I can befriend work. If I feel I have a sure place in life, then work has a place in my life, no more and no less. If I feel that I belong in this world—not alienated or estranged—it is easier to feel that my work belongs to me; it is a natural part of me, not an enemy to be appeased or tamed. If I can feel good about myself getting up in the morning, I can feel good about myself getting up and going to work; I don't need to try to wait for the work to *make* me feel good and be disappointed when it doesn't. If I feel somehow engaged, partnered, caught up in participating in the sweep of life and history and events—if I feel there is a script in which I have an important role—then I don't turn to work to make me feel engaged, to give me my script.

Work becomes one place of many in which I play out who I am, rather than the place in which I discover and prove who I am. Work is not fraught with the power to make or break me; succeeding or failing at work, being appreciated or disappointed over work, is just that, not more. Work no longer has power either to exalt or to debase unduly. Work cannot sweeten or sour life in any significant way, because life has been made immune from the ravages of work and its attempt to deliver mortal blows. I can play at work, as I can play with my children and play with my wife. No life-or-death consequences follow from anything I say or do at work or at home. Nothing has to be just "right." I can do what I feel like doing, without checking for rules and monitors and calculated outcomes. Just as I can hug or explode or experiment at home with wife or kids and know that they and I and our relationship are resilient, steady, and sustained, empowered far beyond my capacity to make or break, so at work I can be experimental or impulsive or playful, because I know that the worst damage I can sustain at work is hardly life-threatening. I even discover that the energy and freedom of my "playful" work often produces better results—in case anyone is still counting—than my more fevered and calculated and measured workmanlike approach.

Since I do not need to be so careful to make it come out right, I can be not only more playful but more companionable at work. If I can befriend work, I can befriend colleagues. If work is not the desperate, scrambling effort to win when most lose, to be right when wrong is so easy, to claim scarce resources, then I need not be so competitive. We really are a team.

That is my portrait of the liberated man at work, my dream for myself and for you.

Liberating the Work Ethic

The first two boys with the rope, the ones who need to make it a tug-of-war, you and I, are victims of the infamous Protestant ethic, the work ethic. As Protestants of four centuries ago threw off the sureties of traditional doctrines and sacraments—threw them off for the distortions they contained and the confinements they imposed—these new Protestants felt naked, helpless, before the now-disclosed and newly deserved wrathfulness of God and before the threatened disasters of life. Largely bereft of the traditional assurances of institution and community, on their own—like the lonely adventurer facing the Western frontier they often were—they were quick to draw on what they could—namely, their own individual efforts—and to decide that their own hard work was their best link with God and salvation. Working hard became a sure sign of God's favor, a sure way to earn God's approval.

How hard was hard enough? A calculus was needed, and the surest measure was competitive comparison. If my hard work yields grander rewards than yours, it must be more satisfactory to God than yours. A short few hundred years later, we still use the same formula whenever somebody hands us a rope, draws a line, and offers us nickels. We may use different language for "God," and "salvation," as we try to give voice to our sense of our own ultimate destiny and welfare. But the formula is the same. We feel naked, helpless, and alone, at risk against huge stakes and huge odds; we must become quick-draw artists, drawing on what we can to best others and thereby save ourselves, and that is our own hard work. We tug the knot across the line as best we can and make a few nickels. How many seems unimportant as long as it is more than what somebody else makes.

If the Protestant ethic's notion of work is the one

reliable means and measure of access to God and to standing in the community, notice how we regard those who do not work. Nonworkers are suspect, people such as homemakers, entertainers, athletes, the unemployed, college students, ministers during the week, even the two boys who clean up fifty dollars between them by "playing." They have not earned their way to heaven or social standing, and workers resent their claiming otherwise. They have not faced us in the tug-of-war of hard work, the only thing that counts. The Protestant ethic is hard on nonworkers.

But how much more is the work ethic hard on us, the workers, those who do shoot it out in the show-down of hard work! For we are condemning ourselves, debarring ourselves from whatever heaven we aspire to, sentencing ourselves to a lifetime of hard labor, because the work is never enough, never quite as many nickels as someone else has, sure to go sour.

In the 1500s, about the same time that Protestants were turning from the works of the church to their own daily hard work as the reliable means of connecting with God and earning salvation, a figure appeared in Europe who has stayed with us ever since, the figure of Johann Faust. He was an actual man who soon took his place in the myths and images of Western consciousness, in innumerable stories, including several still-performed operas. In a state of despair over not getting what he wanted out of life—when his whole life was going sour—the Faust of the stories made a deal with the devil that guaranteed the forms of well-being and salvation he wanted. It seemed a straightforward and easy deal, a sure thing, not unlike the deals most of us make with our own hard work. It seemed one-sided at first; he was getting everything and not having to give anything that wasn't natural and easy; just sign on with the devil and everything was his.

The devil seemed a natural ally, almost part of himself. That's the way it seems with us and work: if we just agree to do what comes naturally anyhow, we are going to reap huge benefits. But the devil who seemed an easy servant to Faust finally became a hard master, as all the bounteous gifts evaporated, as Faust became disenchanted with fame, women, and the rest, and the devil claimed Faust's soul for torment. That's not much different from the way our deal with work turns out. Its promised rewards go sour and the servant, the natural ally, becomes demonic master and claims our soul for torment.

That's the story of Faust, a story we all participate in, a reminder of the Protestant ethic that has cast its spell over us so that we approach life as a tug-of-war. Faust is another reminder of the problem, our overcommitment, our idolization of work, the one-sided unthinking deal which goes sour.

Liberation is in turning our backs sharply on this desperate dependence on the devil. The traditional evangelist's call to conversion makes the devil vivid and frightening and something to flee. There's something to that. We need to look squarely at the devil and say, "You *are* the devil. You are not my savior. I only thought you were, but I was wrong. You have no power over me except what I give you, and I refuse any longer to give you anything." What some of us have learned to say to alcohol or other devils masking as saviors, we need to say to this devil: "You are not the solution, you are the problem, and I defy you."

We can have this conversion, can totally turn around our dependent attitude toward work, if we can change our attitude about ourselves and turn that around too. It is the very first scene of Faust, when he feels like a nobody, that needs to be changed. I am not the naked, helpless, inadequate, lonely failed man who needs in desperation to turn to the lure of an overpromising but demonic savior.

The fundamental conversion/liberation is to discover about myself that I am *not* the person I secretly feel myself to be, the imposter masquerading as a man. I am a man.

In the Faust story, the devil plays on the depressed state in which he finds Faust, the sense of meaninglessness, emptiness, loneliness, the sense of being a discard, failure, reject, fake, the sense that life has passed him by and he has missed the boat. The devil exploits this mood, the mood any man knows. He exploits this mood with the promise of an easy fix. Faust says, "Make it happen for me and I'll do anything. I've got nothing to lose. You are the one who has the power. I've got nothing unless I can get it from you." That's Faust's mood. That's the mood of men when they sell out—to Mephistopheles, to demon rum, to demon work. "I've got nothing to lose. You have the power. I have nothing unless I can get it from you."

That's the mood of all oppressed people, trying to overcome depression by succumbing to oppression, going along with the oppression by casting themselves as powerless and weak and by endowing another with power. Racial and ethnic minorities, many of them, now understand how they accorded power to others by consigning themselves to be nothing. (Oppressor groups are quick to encourage this deferential assignment of power, but the pact works only when the oppressed sign on.) This is what women have discovered about the ways they have let men exercise power over their lives. It's fatal to see oneself as down, needy, empty, and the other as powerful provider: the self as the problem and the other as the solution.

This is also the terrible secret of men; behind the swagger, behind the one-sided love affair with work, behind the reliance on work and working to provide, behind the posturing that our work proves us strong, there is that well-kept, not so well-kept, secret that men have turned to their work out of fear that without it they are nothing.

The liberation from the enslaving pact with the oppressor, whoever and whatever the oppressor, is in the conversion from the feeling of emptiness and nothingness. Not the replacement of one savior by another, one pact by another, one idol by another, one job by another, work replaced by sex or alcohol or golf. Liberation is in the much more radical conversion to feeling no longer needy, no longer hungry for the fix—the conversion to feeling sturdy, resourced, upright, empowered from within and not from outside, not from being without, not from any beings without. Faust never stood up and confronted the devil: "I am a man and you are only a devil." He looked for power and well-being from the hands of the devil, because he thought he had none of his own. That's how he lost his soul. So with most men and work.

The Faust story recalls the story of another man, who did confront the devil, one who must have felt more sturdy, more resourced, less empty than Faust, one who must have felt turned around from all that, converted.

> Then the Devil took Jesus to a very high mountain and showed him all the kingdoms of the world in all their greatness. "All this I will give you," the Devil said, "if you kneel down and worship me."
> Then Jesus answered, "Go away, Satan!" (Matt. 4:8–10a).

"Go away, Satan." Probably the most direct, abrupt, slangy words heard from Jesus, also translatable as "Be off" or (in the King James Version's effort at street talk) "Get thee hence," or even "Get lost" or "Scram." This is not the way one defers to a person of power. These are not the words of a man surrendering control over his own life because he feels too weak or insignificant to claim it, too unsure

of resources or status. These are not the words of
one who needs to buy "the kingdoms of the world"
at any price. These are not the words of someone
small talking to someone big. These are the words
of someone big speaking to someone small. "Go
away." These are words one uses to a pest who has
outlasted your patience, to a buzzing fly, to a tedious
TV commercial, to a boxful of junk mail, to a kid
brother. "Go away, Satan." These are the words of
somebody who has enough going for him that he
does not have to pause before the alluring offer.
These are the words of a liberated man, cutting his
own swath through life, bypassing those whom others would defer to. This is the man who can speak
his mind on the job, set his own pace, wear comfortable clothes to work, even quit his job when he
needs to, expect the disappointments the work
brings, and not feel any less his own man.

In Jesus' story, these are, in fact, the words of
someone who has just had a renewing experience, a
conversion, a baptism. These are the words of someone who has just heard a voice from heaven saying,
"This is my own dear Son, with whom I am pleased"
(Matt. 3:17). That could do a lot toward making
someone feel enough of a somebody to be immune
to a devil's offer. These are the words of someone
who knows he can confront the Devil in trust. "Then
the Devil left Jesus; and angels came and helped
him" (Matt. 4:11). These are the words of someone
launching an energetic and courageous career.

These might be the words of someone who feels
jaunty enough about a fresh spring day, or a new
heart-tingling love affair, or—since spring days and
love affairs don't last too long—someone who feels
securely grounded and sustained in a family or in a
faith. These are the words of someone who doesn't
need to make his own way through life but feels his
way already made for him. These are not the words
of someone who will be chagrined and disgruntled

when the devil's promises fail; he never believed them in the first place; he didn't need to. "Go away, Satan." These are the words of someone who has been converted about how he feels about himself. These are the words of a liberated man.

Liberation as Dance

Andy has a story to tell about a kind of conversion, a kind of liberation, a time when he discovered what it meant to shift from the vigilant and constricted postures of working to the trusting and open postures of being, of living, of loving.

"The other week I think I danced for the first time in my life, really danced like Zorba the Greek. My wife and I were invited to a birthday supper at a Greek restaurant. The food was great, and a combo played music for dancing. The waitresses started it, and everybody joined in, arms on one another's shoulders, making this big circle all around the room. My wife said, 'Let's go.' But I watched until I thought I had the steps figured out. I didn't want to go out there and make a fool of myself. It wasn't all that hard, sort of a 'step, step, step, kick, step, kick.'

"So I got up and broke into the line and started dancing. I got the steps right, better than some of the others. In fact, I got annoyed at some of the people who were messing up the line. I had to sort of pull on the hand of the woman next to me to get her to keep in step, and another woman down the line was also messing up, so I tried to catch her eye and bob my head up and down to count out the steps.

"Then I noticed something else about Greek dancing. The waitresses in the lead were all holding their shoulders level, and most of the rest of us were bouncing up and down. So I began to try to hold my shoulders level, and I began using some body English on the people on each side of me to try to get

them to hold down the bounce. So I was really into
this Greek dancing. But I still didn't feel very grace-
ful."

"Sounds like you were really working hard at it,"
someone observes. "You're being careful not to
make mistakes, you're competing with others, and
you're trying to stay in charge of others and make
the whole thing come out right. That's work."

Andy agrees.

"Exactly. I was going through the motions, but I
wasn't *dancing*. Dancing is letting go of all that,
letting go of trying to move right and move others.
Dancing is letting the music move *you*. You have to
be danced. You have to give up the big 'I,' your self-
consciousness, the feeling that you've got a lot to
gain and a lot to lose and a lot to do, and that
everyone is watching you and quick to criticize or
to praise.

"Something like that happened to me while I was
out there dancing. First I noticed that most everybody else seemed to be happy and I wasn't. They
were looking around and smiling at each other and
bouncing, and I was staring down at my feet. They
didn't seem to care whether I was grim, whether I
got all the steps right—I seemed to be doing enough
worrying for everybody about that.

"Then I realized that the important thing for them
was that we were part of a group and part of the
music, and suddenly I felt that way too. That was a
very different feeling. It was strange, but I liked it. I
was part of this circle and we were moving together
with each other and with the music. They were
there, and the music was *there*. I just had to lean into
it. I felt floating, buoyed. Maybe the wine helped me
let go of that sense of having to make things right. I
was astounded. All of a sudden, it really didn't matter whether I made any 'mistakes.' Who was counting?

"I knew something different was going on when

the music changed and the dance steps changed, and I didn't head for our table to check out the new steps from a position of safety. I stayed in the circle. I was one of them.

"I didn't really get scared until I sat down again and thought, My God, what was I doing? Had I looked foolish? But out there on the floor, I really let go. It didn't seem like me, but then in a funny way it did seem like me, the real me. It really felt good. I would like to have that feeling more."

As in any other conversion, suddenly Andy's view of himself changed from black-and-white to color, from a two-dimensional picture he could look *at*, and maybe try to get into, to a lush scene in which he felt fully embedded and participating. As in any other conversion, the way you think about yourself and your world suddenly changes. It's something like those pictures you can see as either one vase or two faces. The picture just flips from one to the other. The main thing about the conversion is that as the gestalt changes, you change from being in the background, or on the sidelines, to being in the foreground. Conversion is changing *how* you see yourself and the world, *how* you see yourself *in* the world.

"When I go into somebody's kitchen to work out cabinets and cupboards," Andy continues, "I don't try to impose the plan on it, like saying, 'Will the stuff I built in the last kitchen fit in here?' That *would* be work! I look around the kitchen and ask what the arrangement seems to invite. Where does this kitchen want counters and cupboards and the appliances? Every one is different, has its own message to be listened to. It's like dancing.

"I wonder if there is some way to feel that way at my desk. When I am making decisions about buying or hiring or estimating new jobs, I have the feeling that something disastrous will happen unless I personally prevent it. I wonder if I could come to feel that I am part of a process that is carrying itself along, and can even carry me along. Can I trust it?

"Actually, a purchasing decision does make itself, if I could only let go and recognize that. All the facts about comparative specifications and prices and quality and availability—all those facts have their own power and integrity and validity. They can tell me the decision. Same with making estimates or picking new employees and everything else. But it's awfully hard to let go and let those decisions make themselves. It's awfully hard to understand that a mistake is also part of the process, a 'learning experience' in a very important sense of that term.

"That reminds me of junior high school. I got into woodworking because I felt more comfortable down there in the shop than I did upstairs at the desks where somebody was always making me feel that I didn't ever give them back the answers just the way they wanted them. I could never seem to win in the schoolwork. But down in shop it was like I never really could lose, no matter what happened. The shop teacher made it clear that he expected mistakes, wasn't upset by them, that they were part of learning, maybe even the most important part. He would just laugh and say, 'Now you see what happens when you do it that way. Maybe you want to try doing it a different way next time.' And he was right. I could just plunge ahead and feel it was okay 'to do my own thing,' and pretty soon my own thing got to be pretty good."

Len jumps in at this point. He doesn't connect Andy's reflections with his own addiction to desk work. But he does say, "It's my kids that I want to be able to trust more than I do. I'm still hovering around them all the time, doing to them what your classroom teachers were doing to you—and I want to be more like your shop teacher. I'm always warning them, trying to save them from mistakes, and scold them when they make them. I don't want them to do that again! So I work very hard at trying to be a father and make them work very hard at getting along with me. I would like to trust that they are living life the way they need to. They really are good kids—they don't get into any serious trouble. I need to trust that if they are doing things different from the way I would, they're still going to come out all right. I'd like to be enjoying them, not *working* them over all the time; sharing grace, not passing along to them my fear of the law."

Andy's story makes Cliff want to tell of a moment very important to him when he says he learned something important just because he let himself become vulnerable and took a risk. "A couple of months ago, just after they took my friend Art to the hospital with his heart attack, I went over to visit him. He was pretty bad off; as it turned out, he died a couple of weeks later. All the way over to the hospital I was—you know—*working* at the visit." (We remember Cliff working at chopping all the ice off his neighbors' sidewalk.) "I wanted to say the right things that would be good for Art, and I knew my wife was going to ask me when I got home how it went—maybe something like your school teachers, Andy. I didn't know whether I ought to pray with him or what. I thought this might be the last time I ever saw him, and I wanted it to go right.

"But once I got in the hospital, it all seemed different. I was really overwhelmed with seeing Art lying there looking like death. This was totally out of my league. There wasn't anything I could say that would be right or helpful. I was hit so hard by what was happening to Art that I guess I forgot even to think about myself. I lost the feeling that people are looking at me to see how I'm doing. I guess you could say I let myself be danced. I just grabbed Art's hand and hung on to it and didn't let go, and I was trembling, and my eyes teared up.

"I couldn't think of anything to say, and that seemed OK. I just felt how lousy Art must feel,

instead of how uncomfortable I was. After a while
Art whispered 'Thanks,' and we started talking softly
with each other, but then it was real natural. I don't
even know what we said. When I went home it
seemed like I had been carried along by the situation, just as soon as I let go and stopped trying to
take charge. There really was some kind of strength
given to me which I could pass along, once I stopped
trying to manufacture it."

Joseph has his own testimony to give here, and so
does Aaron. Every time Joseph thought he was managing the situation, he would get knocked down, a
kind of enforced vulnerability, and that's where he
found new resources given to him. He was sold into
exile in Egypt and then found himself in jail there.
So he began dealing in dreams, his and others'—as
though everything more "real" had been snatched
away from him and that was all he had left. And it
turned out he parlayed his dream interpretations
into a rather impressive career. But after this career
unwittingly led the entire Hebrew people into exile
and captivity in Egypt, it was time to get them out.
And here is where Aaron and his brother impro-
vised, with his staff turning into a writhing snake,
and other such spectaculars which startled him fully
as much as they did the Egyptians.

We are talking here about what is probably the
most fundamental and most outrageous claim of
Christianity—the claim that God confronts people
especially resourcefully in their moments of feeling
most lost, most beside themselves, most out of the
action, most vulnerable: the claim of the power of
the cross, the claim of renewal precisely and especially in the moments of deepest alienation, alienation of the kind we acknowledged in chapter 1 and
celebrate and welcome here.

The last chapter will look back at each of the
kinds of grief we mentioned in the first chapter and
find how it carries its own healing and liberation.

5

I Am More than a Worker

Most everyone has heard of the French philosopher René Descartes and his famous formula, "I think, therefore I am." It's a chilling premise, to base personal existence on rationality, as though living is not more than thinking. But no more chilling than the stern premise most of us men adopt: "I work, therefore I am."

Who am I? I am worker. If I am not working, I am nobody. The dehumanizing humiliation of the unemployment line is no more real than what many of us experience when stripped of work— hence, stripped of the sense of selfhood—by a weekend, by a vacation, by retirement, or by an intensely human encounter, as with love or with death, in which "working" is of no avail. I am worker. If I am not worker, when I am not worker, I am nobody.

The truth is that I am someone who sometimes works and who sometimes doesn't work; sometimes I even dance. Whether I am working or not working, I am still someone. That is the truth. But it is a truth most of us have great difficulty believing. We have too steadfastly learned that "I am worker."

The conversion I need, the conversion I want— the conversion I fear—is just that change in self-perception: from "I am worker" to "I am someone who sometimes works." This is a wrenching move few of us can make easily, because to get to "I am someone" I must first give up "I am worker," and that means giving up the very identity I have clung to. The conversion requires that anguished descent into hell, that stripping of identifying uniform into a nakedness that feels utterly vulnerable. If I am not worker, I am no one. "Lose yourself to find yourself" means that for me to discover the sense of a sturdy independent selfhood, I must first abandon the only sense of selfhood I have. To think of myself as a good scout, a loyal worker, a successful achiever may be false and self-destructive. But if it is the only self-image I have, it is a lot to give up. It feels that without "I am worker" I am nobody.

This puts us right back into the identity crisis of adolescence, the primordial turmoil and vulnerability from which we once escaped by turning to work as identity-giver. Conversion from "I am worker" risks the pain of adolescent emptiness, feeling again a misfit, lost, unconnected with anything, a monumental orphan.

To fill that emptiness the first time, to give the lostness direction, many of us fastened onto work as the savior. So long as we could plot a career and pursue it, so long as we could check off a day's accomplishment, a week's, cash the paycheck, compile the résumé, keep conversation going with shop-talk, be introduced to strangers with a name of a vocation ("Who are you?" "I am a lawyer . . . engineer . . . purchasing agent"), we thought we were somebody. When the work goes sour, when it does not make us into *somebody* as it had seemed to promise, then the small boy still within us calls out, "The emperor has no clothes!" The painful nakedness is the necessary first step toward discovering the confident nakedness: I *am* somebody even without my uniform of worker, a uniform that turns out to be mask and charade.

Where men have turned to work to give identity

and worth, women traditionally have turned to another person, usually husband. This is important, because women may be able to teach men something about conversion and liberation. As adolescents, women typically were made to feel that they were nobody until they had a man. ("Who are you?" "I am going out with John" or "I am Mrs. John Jones.") Identity and worth derived from the man in her life. Today, women are discovering that this dependence goes sour, this identity is a veneer identity, and women need to discover their identity and worth stripped of their male partners. Some say, "You're asking us to give up our very selves, what we've given our lives to." And they are right: painful nakedness is a prelude to conversion and liberation. Others say, "We need to give up our dependence on men as a bondage to a false and enslaving identity." And they are right, for liberation and new selfhood does rebound from this rock-bottom emptiness and loss. Those are the rhythms of conversion, just as surely among modern women's liberation groups— who would surely be astounded to discover the kinship—as in nineteenth-century frontier evangelistic tent revivals.

Women are discovering that once a woman doesn't *need* a man, is no longer *dependent* on a relationship for identity, there is then a freedom to relate to men with choice and zest and delight. "If I don't *need* a man, then I may *want* him, and I can enter into the relationship with much more of me, more energy, more wholeness, more maturity, more delight and satisfaction." That's what women are learning about a new kind of life. That's what men can learn about how they approach work, once they feel it as partner, not sovereign, as something they feel bigger than, not smaller than, as something just "there," not something they feel swallowed by. When I don't *need* the work (just as when I don't *need* another person), it doesn't have power over

me. A relationship between two people based on need is a relationship based on power and therefore a relationship that breeds intense and souring power struggles. So with our relationship with work. A relationship based on mutual strength and on freedom of choice ("I want you for who you are, not for what you can do for me") is a relationship of delight and exploration and of expanding possibilities. So with the relationship with work.

Men, too, know something about depending on a lover or spouse to make life seem complete, and something about liberating themselves from dependence on women, especially dependence on longing for the perfect woman. It is when we let ourselves feel incomplete or small or empty that we let ourselves feel that the right woman (or the right job) can make it all right. Change comes with the rhythms of conversion: (1) abandon the crutch, the idol, which we have assigned to purvey identity, but which cannot; (2) experience the raw vulnerability and the seeming lack of identity that one is left with after giving up the idol; (3) discover in that emptiness, that lostness—for grace comes most readily *in* just such vulnerability and openness—surprising and unexpected and welcome new sources of identity, energy, and direction, previously crowded out by the addictive "needy" dependence.

Cliff understands it this way: "The other night I saw a lovely sunset and my first thought was, If I could only share this with my wife, it would be perfect. I kept trying to enjoy the sunset, but I kept turning to look for her. It didn't seem really like a sunset without her to point it out to. But then I had another thought which felt really good: Maybe God means this sunset just for me, a private show. Would God do that just for me? Maybe so. It seemed strange at first to stand there and soak in the sunset without *doing* anything about it. And when I did tell my wife about it later, it wasn't pushy like it might have been if she had been there and I had been saying, 'Look there. See that red cloud? See those stripes there?' She said my voice was an octave lower and I seemed peaceful like I had had a religious experience."

Len remembers a similar experience with his wife. "I was reading the newspaper in the morning and came across this funny story. I read it to her. But I guess she was preoccupied or something and didn't respond. She usually has this kind of giggly way of hearing a funny story that makes me relax and laugh at it harder myself. But this time she just didn't say anything, and at first I felt lonely and foolish and abandoned. Just a little. Then I thought, That's OK. It was OK for her to be distracted. And even more important, it was OK for me to enjoy my paper my way."

That is a kind of conversion or liberation experience for Len. Let's hope he'll soon be able to tell us about a similar conversion liberating him from depending on the papers of work.

Paul remembers a love note he once sent his wife, something like this:

> You—and us—mean more to me than anything.
> Tell me that I—and we—mean that much to you.
> I want so hard, I try so hard to please you.
> I need to know that we are OK. Are we?

"I don't think I want to send that to her any more," Paul says, "or to Ronnie or to my boss or to anybody. Trying to please them never really works and never really makes me feel sure of myself. I guess the thing is to feel sure of myself first. Then I stand a greater chance of pleasing them, don't I?"

In a man's love affair with his work, he puts the job on the same pedestal others reserve for a woman. The work is the perfect woman to come whose partnership, whose supportive response, will make his day, make his life, make him a man. If only: If only my work were different . . . the work I expect to be having next year . . . the work I dreamed about when I started out . . . the kind of work **X** has . . . work that is suitable . . . the work they promised me when I started. The search for the perfect job can be as haunting, as unending, as hope-filled, and as devastating as the search for the perfect woman. Expecting the work to be a partner that will give energy, satisfaction, make the day, make one's life seem more complete—this is the illusion, this is the neediness, this is the backwardness that it would be to need a woman to share the sunset with.

In my conversion, I give up expecting or pretending that my job gives me something, makes me somebody, and that I need this. Instead I discover I am somebody who has something to give to the job. The *urgency* about getting the job completed, getting the promotion, compiling the résumé, earning the points, completing the checklist—the urgency disappears when one discovers that he is somebody who can walk into these things freely but does not need them. He can walk out again too—or even have them walk out on him—without feeling chagrin or shame or any other lessening of himself. Urgency is dissolved by trust, fear by grace. He can take his work and its rewards for what they *are*. He can also be realistic—not wishful, not disappointed and angry—about what they are *not*. He does not need to pretend or maneuver them into being more than they are.

From Pain to Liberation

In the first chapter we looked at some of the names we give to the pain work brings us. In these metaphors for the pain, are there also hints for conversion?

Burned Out: Waiting for Fuel and Spark

When we feel burned out, we feel as though the fuel we were once loaded with is all spent, as though the spark that would light the fuel is out, the fuse squelched, the pilot light extinguished. Nothing can get us up and going again.

What this teaches us is how much we depend on something outside of ourselves to keep us fueled, keep us burning, keep us going. Like a rundown wind-up toy, we are waiting to be wound up again, to be turned on again, to have our fuel tank filled again. All this points to the energy we expect from somewhere else, outside of ourselves.

The conversion: Discover and trust the energy sources within oneself which replenish and guide. I am not so helpless or so worthless that I need to wait for somebody else's spark or fuel to turn me on and get me going.

Paul discovers that there is something *he* wants to do on Saturday afternoon—he goes fishing—and his own genuine enthusiasm actually becomes contagious and *attracts* Ronnie.

Cliff decides what *he* wants to talk about at a committee meeting and finds a chance to do that, not apologetic about the agenda and fitting into that, and the committee becomes alive and fueled by him, not vice versa.

Pushing a Stone Uphill: Outsmarting Ourselves Trying Too Hard

No matter how high, how hard, how well we push the stone, there is always farther to go. In fact, the work we are doing seems to multiply itself, so that the more we do, the more we make for ourselves to do. Once we take responsibility for pushing the stone uphill, there is no escape. It will never get to the top, and until it does, we can never let go. Once Len and Andy start making paperwork, pushing papers uphill, paperwork requires more paperwork to keep it going, an endless chain: copies of each paper so all are informed, copy machines, rules for using the copy machines, rules for distributing the copies, forms for acknowledging the copies. . . .

What this teaches us is how easily we let our work become our master, how easily we give our work the energy and initiative, just like the rock ahead of us uphill that we can't let go of.

The conversion: Climb the hill without that rock. Find another rock to chock it and keep it from crashing down and then let go. Find your own path up the hill. Chris should let the Johnsons shovel their own walk, or ask them if they want it shoveled. Do the paperwork as a hobby, with your left hand, so to speak. Let your energy and imagination vault these chores. Let your thoughts while driving and shaving be given to discerning visions and calling of your choosing and rechoosing, not leashed to devices of your own manufacture turned monstrous—that infernal rock.

Discounted: Appraised at Less than Full Value, Less than Promised

When we feel discounted, we feel like a piece of marked-down merchandise in a department store. It's supposed to be worth so much, but that "established" value is crossed out, and the actual value is less. "When they hired me, they promised they would use the particular talents I have, but they don't."

The lesson that feeling discounted teaches us is that we have fallen victim to evaluating ourselves by other people's promises and criteria. It is as though a supermarket stocker has slapped a price tag on us, and we believe it. So when it turns out that they don't mean and don't keep their promises of evaluating us—in institutional life, "they" seldom do—then, of course, we don't feel we measure up. We have sold out to their view of us, their values. So when they discount, we feel really discounted.

The conversion: Discover and trust our own set of values, independent of "theirs." Take the job, begin the day, pursue the career, appraising realistically how you will and will not be good for the work and, just as important, how the work will and will not be good for you. Say these things out loud to yourself. Say them out loud to your fellow workers. Say them out loud, if the question comes up, to your boss. Your judgments of your worth, then, have to do with this contract you make with yourself. You are not lured into taking very seriously whatever initial mark-up promises or eventual markdown discounts "they" make. Their statements are their business, their problem, not yours. When the discounting signals come in, you know that has to do with them, not with you. You can say it is just the way that bosses and businesses and institutions are; they are discounters. That may have something to do with how you feel about the institution. But it doesn't have anything to do with how you feel about yourself.

Cliff can decide how much of the Johnsons' walk he wants to shovel and how thoroughly, according to how much *he* wants the exercise or wants to feel good by doing a favor. He doesn't do it for the Johnsons' appreciation, and he doesn't feel discounted if the Johnsons' appreciation turns out to be ambiguous and lukewarm. Similarly, Ronnie doesn't have any power to make his father feel discounted if Paul doesn't need and assume a "markup" evaluation from Ronnie. Kite flying has its own intrinsic value.

(Of course, sometimes with my boss, there are practical negotiating issues such as salary and definition of responsibilities. But these issues are quite separate from issues of letting myself be valued and discounted, and, indeed, I can approach these negotiating issues much more effectively—more like the second pair of boys with the rope—if my sense of worth is based on my own valuation, not subject to another's discounting.)

As always, such conversion risks a great emptiness. When we give up the badges of the sales ticket slapped on us so as not to make us vulnerable to discounting, we make ourselves immediately vulnerable to much more: to the loss of any badge of value. As with all conversion, first we have to give up the false identity, "their" price tags; then, after the emptiness, find our own. Those are the rhythms of conversion and liberation.

Workaholic: Teased Into the Endless Chase

The rhythms of recovery that Alcoholics Anonymous has discovered are very important guides for the treatment of workaholism. The alcoholic is patiently waited out and accompanied while he or she painfully gives up the desperately held but false and misleading claims of strength and identity, such as "I can control my drinking," until finally the crutch of the drink itself is abandoned in a terrifying shudder of nakedness. This experience of going through the bottom, Alcoholics Anonymous has helped us discover, is survivable and necessary. Healing comes in totally depleted vulnerability. Otherwise, it becomes a matter of trying to replace one addiction with another, gin by wine, liquor by women, gambling, work . . . one lie after another, one overblown dependence after another.

This is the lesson for the workaholic: how easy and how futile it is to replace one counterfeit with another, relying on checklists completed, meetings endured, monthly reports, piles of outbound mail and memos, compiled résumés and bibliographies, Christmas bonuses and annual raises, weekly sales figures, new tables of organization and flow charts, stuffed out baskets. The workaholic thinks of these things as the securer of life and the source of well-being. As each one fails, he turns to the next with renewed assurance born of his need. The workaholic is sure that there is something he can *do* to make his life good.

The conversion is to discover that this is not so. Life is not made good by the things one does, by cutting life down into segments that can be mastered and worked on. Life *is* good. Life is a gift, not an achievement. But the workaholic, like the alcoholic, can't discover this until he gives up the feverish efforts of his own on which he is relying to make life good, until he leaves room for surprising grace.

"I want to be able to go to the office in the morning," Len says, "just feeling adventurous, interested and eager to find out what the day holds for me, instead of making long lists in my head as I'm driving to work about everything I have to do that day to make it come out OK."

"There are times at my desk," Andy says, "when I feel way over my head on the paperwork and I want to scream 'help!' and run back to the shop and turn a table leg on the lathe. But if I just give up trying so hard to get on top of all the figures and the papers—like an alcoholic bottoming out, I guess—and if I lean back in my chair and shut my eyes, then I begin to get some perspective and see a pattern and some point to it all. Then it all begins to make sense and sort of flow together and do its own thing. I begin to feel I don't have to do it."

Paul says, "I just wanted to have *fun* with Ronnie, but I couldn't believe it would happen if I didn't plan it all out. But it did."

"Every time I was down at the bottom and helpless," Joseph can remind us, "that's when the dreams came to me and things started to break for me. It was every time I was trying so hard to be 'responsible' and do everything right, trying to do the things that would please my father or please Potiphar—that's when I got into trouble."

Aaron would remind us, "The biggest mistake in my life was when I stopped trusting God to come through and tried to make my own god."

Grief Work

When work goes sour, there is *grief*, just as surely as when you lose a loved one or your health. We know a lot about ways to handle the grief when someone dies. This can help us learn how to handle the grief when our work turns deadening, killing.

The moment of grief is the moment of holding and treasuring simultaneously life *and* death, hope and disappointment, promises trusted and promises shattered. To a man recently widowed, his wife is both very much alive and very much dead. He is aware, constantly and vividly, of her presence. He turns to speak to her, to embrace her; he pours her coffee with his; he makes plans in his head to get away from his present stress by taking a holiday with her. He strokes the clothes in her closet and pores over photograph albums. But at the same time he wipes her out of his life—she is dead. He empties her closets and makes plans to give away all her clothes. He stores away the photograph album, out of sight. He plans a vacation somewhere she never wanted to go and occupies himself with friends and pastimes she never approved of. He buys a large coffee mug, since now he'll be drinking all the coffee from the two-cup drip pot.

An extreme reaction of the first kind—clinging to the wife—founders on the side of denying the death and separation, which is real and undeniable. An extreme reaction on the other side—discarding her memory summarily—founders by denying the life and connection, which remain a very real and undeniable part of the widower's life. Sometimes one or another of these reactions persists for years in its crippling one-sidedness. The healing miracle of grief work, when it happens, as it inevitably must, is in holding together as one reality the life and death, the hope and disappointment, the connection and separation, the trust and betrayal. Somehow, in good grief work, there is simultaneous investment and withdrawal, a claim and a letting go, a yes and a no, both hearty. The widower can enthusiastically recall his life with his wife, and celebrate it, at the same time that he can speak of her death firmly and clearly and get on with planning his life without her. The letting go does not make more timid the celebrative recall, but neither does all that fondness hinder the clear letting go.

I think that healthy, liberated relationships between people, even while both are alive and together, partake of the same kind of good grief work. For death is as actively present in life as life persists in death. In a living relationship, one person fails, disappoints, separates from the other in moments that are as wrenchingly painful and grief-filled as any physical death, maybe more so. A man able to live life and to enter a relationship knows unflinchingly and without dismay that this relationship will fail him in death-dealing ways. But expecting this failure as an inevitable part of any relationship in no way impairs the zest with which he enters the relationship. It's all part of the way things are in this world, just as the hopes and yearning, even the needs, that he invests in the relationship are not allowed to exaggerate the failure, when it happens, into something devastating and catastrophic. It's only a failure in a relationship, part of the natural history of the relationship. So what else is new?

I think the converted man feels sturdy and resilient enough to approach work with the same anticipation. The work will be good for him in many ways, and he for the work, and the work will also be full of painful, souring grief. That's just the way it is. He will engage the work with all the best it deserves, the zest undiminished by his clearheaded recognition that the work is not promising to meet his every need and that it will even disappoint the promises it does make. His zest, if any, will be enhanced by this unveiled realistic perception, for he will be engaging the work objectively for what it is, unclouded by his own fantasies. He will be *conscious* of what the work is and is not. He doesn't have to engage the work with jaded ambivalence, secretly and unconsciously holding back because he unconsciously knows and fears the souring. The work is work, no more—not a saving love partner, not a god—and no less; it deserves the investment of a genuine calling, a work partner.

Because the converted man feels larger than his work and not ultimately dependent on it, he will approach work with a somewhat amused detachment. He will be interested and curious to see how it comes out, passionately interested but not desperate. He will not have a life-or-death urgency about it, because he will recognize that it contains both life and death. He will approach work like an avid TV sports fan or a poker player: he will throw himself into the game, and savor a win, and shrug off a loss, because that is part of the game and because the game is only part of his life, not his whole life. He will throw himself into his work as a scientist throws himself into a new theory, advocating and defending and testing it as vigorously as he can, not in spite of but because he knows the theory is doomed to disproof—that is its purpose, to be tested and to give way to a better theory. The scientist's commitment is to the theory, for both its life and death, but the commitment even more fundamentally is to the process of discovering and testing theories. The theory is part of the process, no more and no less; it deserves all the passion for being part of it, and all of the willingness to let it go because it is only part.

Theologically, this is called justification by faith, and it is what saves working from becoming idolatrous good works. The work is an essential part of life, but only that. It is subject to the same fallenness, the same life-and-deathness, as all the rest of life. It is not the creator or saviour of life that we often try to make it. For that we turn to God, to the God who has especially promised to enter sourness and grief and to recycle it, to embrace death and to reclaim it as part of life, to hold each of us as a dear partner.